Successful Vacation Homes

⌂ Successful Vacation Homes

Ronald Derven
Ellen Rand

Structures Publishing Company
Farmington, Michigan

Manufactured in the United States of America

Edited by Shirley M. Horowitz

Book design by Carey Jean Ferchland

Cover photo by Ernest Brown, courtesy California Redwood Association.

Current Printing (last digit)
10 9 8 7 6 5 4 3 2 1

Structures Publishing Company
Box 1002, Farmington, Mich. 48024

Library of Congress Cataloging in Publicaton Data

Derven, Ronald.
    Successful vacation homes.

    Includes index.
    1. Second homes. I. Rand, Ellen, joint author. II. Title.
TH4835.D47   643   78-31270
ISBN 0-912336-79-X
ISBN 0-912336-80-3 pbk.

Contents

This sensitive vacation home design uses natural surroundings to best advantage without disturbing the setting. Shown here is a McCall, Idaho vacation home designed by architects Heaton & Jones. The angular design is emphasized with redwood siding installed on the diagonal. (Photo by Glen Allison, courtesy of the California Redwood Association)

Introduction

To own land and build a vacation retreat on it is almost everyone's dream. But can that dream be turned into a reality at an affordable cost? We believe that it can. This book is designed to give you basic guidelines in finding and buying property, and then planning, building and financing a vacation home that will prove to be serviceable, economical and emotionally satisfying.

Unquestionably, land and building costs are high and ever-increasing. It has been estimated that land costs double in price every five years, while building material costs have often outstripped the inflation rate. It must be stated at the outset, emphatically, that there are really no "bargains" to be had in buildable land located in desirable beach, mountain, woodland or lake areas; nor are high building costs about to take a nose-dive in the foreseeable future. However, by following guidelines set forth in this book, you will be able to transform your dream vacation home into a reality as economically as possible. It should be noted that if you decide to wait just another few years to start building, future construction and land costs may well outpace any dollars you have saved toward the project.

USING THIS BOOK

BUDGETS

The key to building an affordable vacation home is to realistically scale your design and material preferences and interior space requirements to suit your budget. Throughout the book, you will find the theme "Smaller is Better." You may be surprised to find that your needs can be comfortably accommodated in a home of less than 500 sq. ft.! Or that a parcel of land that is within walking distance of a lake can be thousands of dollars less expensive, and perhaps have better soil drainage. Or that amenities you can't live without in your primary residence, like dishwashers and garbage disposers, become expensive and unnecessary frills in a vacation home.

We point out, too, how to cut down on costs by doing much of the work yourself if you are handy. In fact, an entire chapter (Chapter 5) is dedicated to the do-it-yourselfer interested in building a small home from scratch.

ALTERNATIVES

Another way to achieve savings is to select one of the hundreds of "manufactured" home packages available: precut, prefabricated, modular or mobile homes. You can assemble many of the "shells" of these home packages yourself, with rudimentary building tools. As we point out in Chapter 6, packaged homes can prove advantageous in areas where labor is in short supply, or in cases where the shell must be put up quickly so that work can proceed indoors in inclement weather. You must find out, however, what the "extras" like shipping and interior finishing will cost *before* you choose a packaged home.

ENERGY SAVINGS

We also stress energy conservation strategies throughout the book, and present alternative techniques for heating, cooling and insulating vacation homes for maximum energy efficiency. These basic techniques will also mean reduced operating and maintenance costs over the life of your home.

PLANNING

Clearly, building a vacation home can present more puzzles to you than would a primary residence. Whereas in your primary residence you may not give a second thought to flushing the toilet or turning on a tap for water in the kitchen, these basics must be carefully planned in a vacation home. Then, too, there is the question of dealing with local officials: health department inspectors, planning and zoning boards (in many cases), building inspectors. And, one of the biggest quandaries: how to keep track of progress on your home when, for the most part, you may be hundreds of miles away from it during the day? We address all these issues in the first three chapters of the book.

Despite all these potential headaches, the effort will be worth it. Whether for a single in the city or a suburban family, a vacation home offers more than just a place to "get away from it all." It is a place to entertain friends and share moving experiences with those close to you. It is also a good investment; you can rent it out for some extra income, or you can "swap" it with other homeowners in the U.S. and abroad for a "rent-free" vacation.

We intend this book will give you a realistic view of the pleasures and pains involved, and aid you in overcoming difficulties encountered during the various buying and building stages.

1
Finding a Place in the Country

The enjoyment of your leisure home can be greatly enhanced by recollection of all the excitement—and headaches—involved in creating it. But make no mistake; building a leisure home is not for the faint of heart. It takes a tremendous commitment of time and energy—first in finding a likely spot to build on, and then in conceiving the plan and seeing it through. Patience, flexibility, and a sense of humor when confronted with unexpected calamities, will all stand you in good stead.

EARLY CONSIDERATIONS

Some of the problems that can arise involving the land itself are detailed in this chapter, as well as in Chapter 4. Problems arise, too, during construction, particularly if severe weather halts building progress or if material shortages crop up.

SECURITY

One of the toughest aspects of building a leisure home is how to protect it. Unless you are actually building it yourself ("how-to" in Chapter 5), you are usually too far from your site to oversee daily construction and to keep watch on materials.

Even if you spend all your vacation time and weekends at the site, it's difficult to really gauge how effectively subcontractors are working on your house. If you are a newcomer to the area in which you're building, it is particularly hard to determine whether or not you are paying market rates for labor and materials.

Once the house is finished, you must concern yourself with securing it during the week, or during the seasons when you won't be using it. Vacation homes can be easy prey for burglars and vandals. The home must also be protected against natural invaders like termites, possums, and other creatures, as well as against harsh natural elements like wind, rain, snow, and water. Moisture in both its dramatic and unobtrusive forms can prove to be your home's worst foe—creeping into basement or crawlspace, attics, doors, windows, and rusting out furnaces and water heaters.

ECONOMIC NOTES

Economically, your home can be a problem, too. If at some point you find it impossible to carry the extra cost of owning a leisure home, you may have to think of selling it. And, while a tangible investment that generally appreciates in value at a greater rate than inflation, it is not a "liquid" asset. That is, if you have to sell it *immediately,* chances are you won't get the best price for it.

All this is not to dissuade you from embarking on this major undertaking. Rather, we hope to alert you so that you can avoid these problems.

Vacation homes are perhaps the least documented segment of the housing universe. Average figures on resale values, mortgage requirements, and preferred styles are elusive. Because there is such a tremendous diversity in the kinds of properties (beachfront to mountaintop) and in the kinds of homes built (pre-cut geodesic domes to Swiss-style chalets), generalizations are hard to come by.

WHERE TO BUILD

According to the latest figures available from the *Annual Housing Survey,* a joint publication of the Census Bureau and the Department of Housing and Urban Development, here is a breakdown, regionally, of the vacation home market:

	Vacant, Seasonal, and Migratory	% of Market
Northeast	591,000	38.5%
North Central	424,000	27.6%
South	341,000	22.3%
West	178,000	11.6%

CLIMATE: A Basic Consideration

The design of your house, and the materials used to build it, will be influenced greatly by the climate in the area.

Sunshine.   Coastal areas generally have more cloudiness than interior areas. Mountainous areas have less sunshine than interior areas, while desert areas have the most sunshine of all. During November, December and January, the Pacific Northwest gets about 100 hours of sunshine, while the Great Lakes area gets about 80 to 100 hours. Southeastern California and southern and western Arizona get more than 240 hours of sunshine. In the summer, most of the U.S. gets about 300 hours of sunshine per month. Again, the greatest amount is in southeastern California and western Arizona. The least mean total sunshine is experienced along the Washington and Oregon coasts: 1,800 to 2,200 hours annually.

Humidity.   The amount of moisture in the air can either make you feel hot and uncomfortable in the summer, or cold and clammy in the winter. The preferred indoor relative humidity range is 40 to 60 percent.

Relative humidities are highest in coastal areas where winds blowing inland from water surfaces carry a lot of moisture. Humidity is lowest in deserts and semi-arid Southwest. While Tampa, Fla., may be suffering 88 percent humidity, Yuma, Ariz., would have perhaps 57 percent. The Northeast is generally much more humid than the Southwest.

Wind.   On-shore winds over coastal areas can make those areas milder and moister than winds coming from the interior of the continent. Prevailing winds on the Pacific Coast are from the northwest. Winds over the eastern two-thirds of the country are from the northwest or north during January and February, and generally from south and southwest from May through August. Easterly winds of northeast trades prevail over the Florida peninsula except during December and January, while southerly winds prevail in the Texas-Oklahoma area from March through December.

Fog.   Heavy fog, in which visibility is reduced to ¼ mile or less, occurs on from 80 to 100 days annually in several areas, including: the northern part of the Pacific Coast; along the California coast; in the Olympic and Cascade ranges in the West; in the Appalachians; and along the New England coast.

Floods.   The northern interior and northeast parts of the U.S. get floods most frequently during the spring months, while the Pacific states experience flooding more in the rainy winter months.

Snow.   Mean annual snowfall at the higher elevations in the western mountains ranges from 100 to over 200 inches per year. The Rockies experience more than 10 snow days per year, while the upper Great Lakes region and northwestern Lower Michigan experience 20 to 30 days, as does most of New York and New England, and parts of Virginia, Maryland and Pennsylvania. The east shore of Lake Ontario and northern New Hampshire experience more than 40 days of snow, annually.

Temperature Variations.   Temperatures can vary widely over short distances, especially in mountainous areas. Variations are due to differences in altitude, slope of land, type of soil, vegetative cover, bodies of water, air drainage and urban heat effects. An increase in altitude of 1,000 feet can cause a decrease of 3.3 degrees F. in the average annual temperature of an area.

You can get more specific information on the climate of your chosen area, including precipitation records, humidity, temperatures, wind, fog and other factors, from the U.S. Department of Commerce, Weather Bureau, Climatological Section, National Records Section, Asheville, N.C. 28801. Climate books are published for each state.

CHOOSING THE SITE

Try to locate property within several hours of your primary residence. This means you will spend less time driving back and forth both at the choosing and using stages. Future gasoline crises aside, it's tough to enjoy your leisure time after a too-lengthy drive, and while facing the prospect of a similar drive back. During construction, particularly, you'll be "ferrying" back and forth from the site frequently enough to discourage a very long drive.

Low in square footage, yet functional and dramatic, this home stresses indoor/outdoor living with a deck off the kitchen for dining. Windows are located and designed to let in maximum amount of natural light; the interior chimney is another energy-saver. (Photo courtesy of Champion Building Products)

Once you know what type of property and what area you'd be happiest in, start checking local sources for leads on available acreage. Officers of local lending institutions, classified ads in real estate sections, building supply outlets and town or county officials (town clerks, zoning, planning, building departments) can help.

Area real estate brokers are probably the most well-informed group, vis-a-vis what's on the market and what kinds of prices are currently being commanded for land. A good broker can not only steer you in the direction of the property; he or she can act as the "buffer" in negotiations for purchasing the property, and can suggest methods and sources of financing. But remember that a broker acting as an agent for the seller has the responsibility of selling that property at the best price, quickly. Don't allow yourself to be rushed into a purchase. Don't sign *any* contract or purchase *any* property if there are still unanswered questions.

Some of the points to be answered include:

- Is there a year-round source of water? If a well must be dug, will you have the legal right to *use* that water?

- Is the ground conducive for building? If there is no sewer system, can the soil accommodate a septic system? Is drainage good, or will you have a problem with flooding after a rain storm? Or is the property on a flood plain?

- Can utilities be brought into the site easily? Will the cost of building an access road, bringing in electricity or gas, wipe out economies achieved in buying an out-of-the-way parcel?

- If the property is adjacent to public lands, are there any development plans afoot that would affect the site? Does the town or county plan on building near the site?

- If the property fronts on a country road, does the road provide direct access to a site or is there, perhaps, a ravine fronting on the road?

- What kinds of building restrictions are there? Is there minimum parcel zoning or minimum floor space requirements? Can you build a home for four-season use, or is seasonal use restricted?

- Are there restrictions on architectural style?

- Are any building moratoria in effect? (This affects coastal properties in particular.) Is there any ban on additional gas or sewage hookups?

- Must you submit some form of environmental impact statement to local or state agencies for approval?

- If other properties have to be crossed to get to the site, will you have the legal right to do so? Is such an easement obtainable?

- If others have to cross the site to get to their own properties, will you be disturbed? Can a house be set far enough from the road to prevent any disturbance?

- What are the taxes? Are there any existing liens on the property?

- Is the site within easy reach of police and firemen?

- Are recreational and cultural activities close by? Where are suppliers of basics like groceries and hardware?

- If the property includes a lake, pond or stream, is the water free from contamination?

Do try to see the property under less-than-ideal conditions, such as during an "off-season," or in the rain.

Real estate pros say that location is the most important factor in determining value. Even the pros sometimes make big blunders in location and price when it comes to acquiring property, so you should understand at the outset that finding the right land may be a very painstaking process.

One important point to keep in mind is that land is generally less expensive if you buy several acres, rather than buying one acre or one lot. In the same area, a one-acre parcel might sell for perhaps $7,000, but a six-acre parcel might sell for $27,000, which is the better value in the long run. Moreover, you generally get more value for your dollar if you buy acreage from a landowner directly rather than from a land development company.

In calculating the price of raw land, keep in mind that building a road, bringing in utilities, drilling a well and laying out a septic system can add many thousands of dollars onto the initial cost. Acreage that already has utilities in, but costs more, might be a more desirable alternative. Also, be sure that your purchase depends on getting whatever zoning variances you may need, on getting satisfactory results from soil percolation tests or well samples, and clear title to the property.

A title company, probably engaged by your attorney, must ascertain that the seller, indeed, has the right to sell the property to you. It is also a good idea to have a survey of the property done. This will cost a few hundred dollars, but will save you far more than that in potential legal headaches should there be a question over boundaries at some point in the future. The survey will determine the precise measurements of the land parcel. That description should be included in the contract of sale. It should go without saying that you ought not sign anything until you have spoken to your attorney first.

BUYING THE LAND

Purchasing the property can be done in a number of ways; most vacation area land sales are cash transactions, but you are certainly not restricted to paying all-cash for the property.

One popular method of financing is through the seller. In other words, you pay a substantial downpayment on the property, perhaps 40 to 50 percent, and arrange with the seller to pay off the remainder to him over a specified period of time, at an interest rate that is mutually acceptable. Terms might include interest payments only for a certain period of time, with a "balloon" principal payment at the end of that period. Or, you could arrange a schedule of conventional principal-and-interest payments.

If the seller has a mortgage on the land, you can either buy the property "subject to" the mortgage, or "assume" the loan yourself. In the former method, the seller would still be responsible for making mortgage payments; your downpayment and subsequent monthly payments would reflect this. If you "assume" the mortgage, that means that you are responsible for the monthly payments, at the same terms called for in the seller's mortgage. You would have to work out a mutually acceptable sum to pay the seller, above the existing mortgage.

Some banks don't allow "assumption" of mortgages, mainly because prevailing interest rates are likely to be higher than they were years ago when many loans were made. So, make sure that the lender gives written approval to the seller to transfer the property to you.

There are two stages to go through when buying real estate: signing a contract of sale, and *closing,* at which time title is transferred. The period of time between "going to contract" and "closing" varies, depending on how long you and your attorney think it will take to satisfy all conditions.

When you sign the contract, you will have to put down a certain amount of money as an "earnest money deposit." This is applied to the total agreed-upon amount for the downpayment, or sale price, which you will pay to the seller at the time of closing.

Title is transferred to you by means of a deed. There are several different types of deeds. Try to avoid a quitclaim deed. This merely passes on any title, interest or claim the seller has in the property, without guaranteeing that such title, interest or claim is really valid!

FINANCING

It is likely that you will have to finance a portion of your vacation home. There are a number of ways and a number of sources available, but the question really boils down to this: how much of a monthly payment can you afford on top of your regular budget?

Most manufacturers or dealers of precut or pre-fab homes can help you arrange financing. They can either offer a list of possible sources, or help you with your presentation to the bank of your choice.

If you seek a conventional long-term loan for your house, either through a local savings and loan, savings bank or commercial bank, or through your home town bank, you should be aware that the terms for second homes are considerably stiffer than they are for primary residences. For a second home, a mortgage lender will require a downpayment of up to 50 percent of the purchase price, while the interest rate will be .5 to 1.5 percent higher than it would be for a mortgage on a primary residence. Moreover, a mortgage on a primary home is usually for a period of 25 to 30 years, while a mortgage on a second home is more likely to be for a period of 15 to 20 years.

On a construction loan, the bank will usually charge a fee—a small percentage of the total amount borrowed—for processing and inspection of construction. Funds will be advanced only when the bank has been assured that each stage has been completed satisfactorily.

Bear in mind, too, that if money conditions are tight in the area or in the country generally, bankers are likely to cut down on making loans for vacation homes. They are considered a luxury, not a necessity or a priority item. Regardless of money conditions, your mortgage lender will carefully scrutinize your house plans to make sure they conform to their

One of the "packaged" homes available, its roof overhangs the deck, and carport providing style and shady areas for the owners. (Photo courtesy of Deck Homes Inc.)

standards, and will carefully scrutinize your financial picture to assure themselves that you will be able to meet the mortgage payments.

Unconventional plans do tend to raise eyebrows; the mortgage lender's viewpoint is that in the event of a default on your part, a conventionally styled home would be more marketable for them than would a replica of the Taj Mahal.

If you want a standard construction loan (a short-term loan), you must own your property outright, and you must submit exact plans and specifications to the bank for approval. The interest rate is higher for a construction loan than it would be for long-term financing, and you will probably need to have a licensed contractor to finish the job, to meet the bank's requirements.

Other ways of financing a vacation home are: taking out a personal loan; borrowing on your life insurance; refinancing your existing mortgage, or taking out a second mortgage on your primary residence.

Of these methods, borrowing on life insurance may be preferable. These types of loans do not require that you make monthly payments; but it's a good idea to stay current with the interest charges. Remember, too, that as long as the principal is still outstanding, your insurance policy is reduced by that amount.

Interest rates on personal loans are generally higher than borrowing on life insurance; you may want to consider taking out such a loan to finance the construction of your home, and then applying for a traditional long-term mortgage to pay off the short-term debt. This is one way of financing construction without incurring construction loan fees.

Refinancing an existing mortgage makes the most sense if you have substantial equity in your home; if property values have increased in your primary residence area so that the mortgage can be realistically rewritten for a higher amount; and, if prevailing money rates are not too much higher than they were when you took out the original mortgage. For example, refinancing a mortgage at high interest rates would mean substantially higher monthly payments for you if your original interest rate was much lower.

Second mortgages, like personal loans, vary widely in terms, rates and borrowing limits, from state to state and from bank to bank. But interest rates are generally high: at least three percentage points higher than conventional mortgages. And, since they are relatively short-term loans, that means that monthly payments will be high, too.

Before you choose your finance route, then, sit down with a calculator, pad and pencil and go through *all* the options.

Federal Land Banks. One lesser-known source of financing is through Federal Land Banks. There are 12 Federal Land Banks in the U.S., one in each of the twelve Farm Credit Districts. These Banks make long-term loans secured by first liens on real estate in rural areas through more than 500 local Federal Land Bank Associations.

Though designed primarily to finance individual and corporate farmers and ranchers, the Federal Land Banks do provide long-term loans for individual rural residents, too. To qualify, you cannot have more than one loan outstanding on a rural home at any one time. Nor can the loans be made if you're planning to build a home in order to rent or resell it.

A rural area is defined as being essentially agricultural in character, but may also include towns or villages whose population does not exceed 2,500 people, and which are not adjacent to large population centers. A further restriction is that each Bank is limited in rural home lending to 15 percent of its total loan volume outstanding.

Loans can be made for moderate-priced dwellings that are conventionally built, or are modular in construction, or for mobile homes meeting certain standards. Loan terms are flexible, and there is no prepayment penalty.

For a list of Federal Land Banks, and the territory served by each, see Appendix B.

RENTING OUT AND TAX CONSEQUENCES

At some point you will probably hear that your vacation home will pay for itself if you rent it out during periods when you prefer not to use it yourself. In reality, this is difficult if not impossible, although renting can certainly help defray a portion of the cost of carrying that house.

Before you incorporate renting as part of your vacation home strategy, ask yourself these questions:

- Will you feel comfortable knowing that strangers are in your house? And that extra maintenance and repair will be necessary to keep the house in top condition?

- Do you want to rent the property out during periods when it is most desirable—in the summer, for a beach house, in the winter, for a ski chalet? Or would you prefer to use the home yourself during those periods?

- Is your property really marketable during the seasons you wish to rent it out?

- Is the rent level you have determined as necessary to cover your carrying costs in line with the market? Or is it unrealistically high?

- Can you handle all the details of renting out the house yourself (i.e., advertising through classifieds, announcements in local commercial and retail establishments, "word of mouth"), and effectively "qualify" prospective renters? Or should you retain an area broker or management firm to rent the property for you?

- Will your homeowners insurance policy cover the home and its contents if it is partially used as a rental property?

The tax laws of the U.S. have become considerably more stringent than they used to be regarding vacation homes. Since the Tax Reform Act of 1976, deductions attributable to the rental of a vacation home require that certain standards be met, namely:

(1) the property must be rented for more than 15 days during the year in order for income and expenses to be reportable;

(2) deductions that amount to more than the gross rental income from the property are barred in cases where the owner rents out the home for 15 days or more and uses it for 14 days or more, or more than 10 percent of the number of rental days (whichever is greater).

In other words, you cannot effectively build up deductions such as depreciation greater than the amount of rental income. You can prorate interest and taxes according to rental use, however. Let's assume you've used your summer place for 30 days in one taxable year, and rented it out for 20 days, and that your rent came to $1,100 while your yearly interest and tax bill came to $1,000.

If you offset all $1,000 against the $1,100 income, you would only be allowed an additional $100 for other deductions (including repairs, maintenance, insurance, utilities and depreciation). By offsetting a portion of the interest and taxes against rental income, say 50 percent or $500, you'd still be able to get $600 worth of other deductions. The remaining $500 in interest and taxes can be itemized as personal expenses.

Since tax laws can change with near-whimsical frequency, we advise that you check with an accountant when figuring out how rental of your vacation home affects your tax return.

SWAPPING

As an alternative to renting out your house, you can also "swap" your home with others for a rent-free vacation. There are a number of home-swapping services who have literally thousands of home listings in the U.S. and abroad.

Their directories have pictures of homes available for exchange purposes, plus a brief summary of the homes' features. If you find something intriguing in one of these directories, it makes good sense to write detailed inquiry letters to prospective swap-mates, including photos of your own home and references. Among the home-swapping services are:

Vacation Exchange Club, 350 Broadway, New York City, N.Y. 10013; Inquiline, Box 208, Katonah, N.Y. 10536; Holiday Home Exchange Bureau, Box 555, Grants, N.M. 87020

2
Hiring a Builder, Drawing the Plans

If you are planning to do most of the construction yourself, or will act as your own general contractor, you may ignore this section! Otherwise, it will be crucial to find a contractor who will understand your needs. Although you will not exactly be living with this person, the fact is that you will be in very close communication throughout the course of construction, which could take anywhere from a few months to a year on a conventional, "stick-built" home.

Because you are not likely to be at the site to supervise the proceedings on a day to day basis, it is particularly important for you to have a contractor in whom you have substantial trust. There are always unexpected surprises in the course of construction: weather conditions can play havoc with schedules; materials shortages can delay deliveries and raise prices; subcontractors can fold. It's important that the contractor keep you informed, and that you can believe what he's telling you.

Finding a good builder requires a little research. Good sources include: friends or homeowners in your chosen area; your architect; the builders' association of the state; building supply dealers in the area; lending institutions in the area; or, local real estate brokers.

Pinpoint a few potential candidates, and ask each to give you rough cost estimates for your home. You should be able to give these contractors a pretty clear idea of the type of house you're interested in, the size, number of bedrooms and bathrooms, and types of materials you want to use. Remember that an estimate is *not* a commitment that your house can be built for that amount.

At the same time, it would make sense to check the builders' reputations with past customers. The builders should be willing to provide names. Ask if the work was accomplished within the proposed time frame, if there was sufficient attention to craftsmanship and detail, and whether the builder was easily accessible by phone. The local chamber of commerce and Better Business Bureau might be of assistance at this stage, too.

You should get at least three written bids for a home. These bids would detail your specifications: the scope of the work to be done; materials and supplies required, and complete costs. Make requests to each bidder the same, for comparative purposes. Set a time limit for receiving written bids. Three weeks to a month would be realistic. Don't assume that the lowest bid means the best "deal" for you. Aim for quality, too.

Once you have selected a builder, a written agreement should be drawn up detailing the work involved and the payment schedule. Provision should also be made for an escrow account: that is, you will hold a certain portion of the final payment aside in case the work has not been completed to your satisfaction. Payment would be made when the work is completed to your satisfaction.

Payment schedules usually call for partial payment upon completion of a certain amount of work, and other payments in stages as other phases of work are completed.

Look over the final bills with a keen eye. More than one "city slicker" has paid more than he should for work and materials in country homes!

ACTING AS YOUR OWN CONTRACTOR

If you are acting as your own contractor, setting up a payment schedule will be somewhat different. For carpenters who are going to be spending a long time on the job, it might make sense for you to establish credit at the local lumber yard or building supply outlet. This way, the carpenter can order the materials and charge them to your account. This will give you an accurate record of the quantity and price of materials ordered. You would then have to pay the carpenters for their labor, calculated on an hourly basis.

Vacation homes should be designed for minimum maintenance, as is this California beach house designed by architect George Klett. Redwood siding need not be painted; vegetation around house is left in its natural state. These features help keep maintenance effort low. (Photo by Karl Rick, courtesy of the California Redwood Association)

Before work proceeds, come to an agreement about the timing of payment: whether it be weekly, twice a month, once a month, once every two months or whatever is mutually agreeable.

Other mechanics, such as plumbers, electricians and masons, won't be spending as much time on your job as the carpenters. They will submit bills to you upon completion of their work, calculated on their hourly rate plus the cost of materials. Often these tradesmen will want to work for a set contract price which includes time, materials, profit and overhead.

A rule of thumb is that labor will comprise about half the cost of building your house, which is one reason why it makes sense to do much of the work yourself, if you have the time and inclination.

Another rule of thumb is that it will take approximately twice the amount of money or more to build a home as it did to purchase the land beneath it.

You can assume that total construction costs for conventionally built homes will be about $35 to $50 per square foot. If you want to build a 1,000 square foot house, then, you can estimate that your construction costs will be $35,000 to $50,000, exclusive of land. Of course, price depends on more than square footage. A 1,000 square foot log cabin in a field will not cost nearly as much as a slick 1,000 square foot contemporary home overhanging a cliff.

HOW TO READ BUILDING PLANS

Whether you are building the house yourself or having a contractor do it for you, understanding how to read building plans will give you a firm grasp on what must be done.

TYPES OF PLANS

For the typical single-family house, plans are broken down as follows: plot or site plan; foundation plan; floor plans; elevation plans; and mechanical plans.

Plot or site plan. This shows the contours, boundaries, roads, utilities, significant physical features, large trees and other structures on the site. Usually the surveyor will draw up the plan, which is then submitted to the architect. The architect in turn will design the structure and fit it on the survey. This plan takes zoning setbacks into account. Because existing elevations are also shown as contour lines, it allows you and the excavator to see how much earth must be moved.

Foundation plan. This plan shows the main foundation of the house, as well as locations of piers. It also details the type of footing and concrete block wall to be constructed. This plan will detail any waste or vent pipe which will go from the house to the outside. All dimensions are shown.

Floor plans. This can be a single sheet of paper or many sheets of paper, depending on the size of the house. A small cabin, for example, would only take one sheet whereas a three-story structure generally takes three or more sheets. Included in the floor plans are dimensions, location of windows and doors, location of walls and partitions, character of materials to be used, and more.

Framing plans. These show the dimensions and arrangement of structural members. Often the floor framing plan is superimposed on the foundation plan to show sill plate, joist size and location and bridging. The wall framing plan is quite similar in what it shows. That plan details the vertical plane of the house, whereas the floor plan details the horizontal. Typically shown are studs, bracing, sill, plates, posts and other structural members. Roof-framing plan gives similar information regarding that structure.

Utility plan. This plan details where utilities enter the house, location of electrical outlets and fixtures.

Mechanical plan. If the house is large enough, the mechanical plan will detail where heating ducts are to be placed, location of furnace, hot water heater and other mechanical equipment.

Elevations. These will probably be of greatest interest to you. These show you in pictures what the house will look like. In fact, the intent of these architectural drawings is to communicate the scope of the house, in pictures.

Cross-sections. Often plans will detail various cross-sections—cuts of a vertical plan. On the foundation plan, there may be a cross-section of the concrete footing and foundation wall. Cross-section plans can detail other elements of the house as well.

Details. Often the above-mentioned drawings cannot accurately communicate a particular detail of the house. Therefore, the architect draws a very specific sketch of what he wants. This might be a particular wall section, interior stairs or a deck railing.

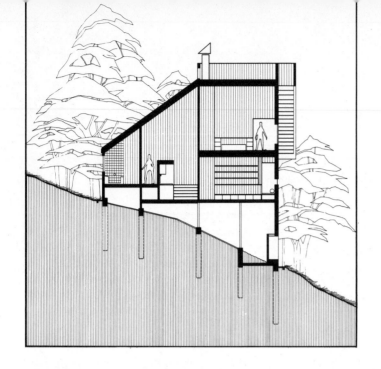

Architects' drawings are designed to communicate what a house will look like. Illustrative tools are elevations, floor plans and contour drawings. Shown here are plans and the completed house, designed by architects McCue, Boone and Tomsick. The Tiburon, California house takes advantage of steep site and natural breezes in unusual "spiral within a square" plan. (Photo by Jeremiah O. Bragstad)

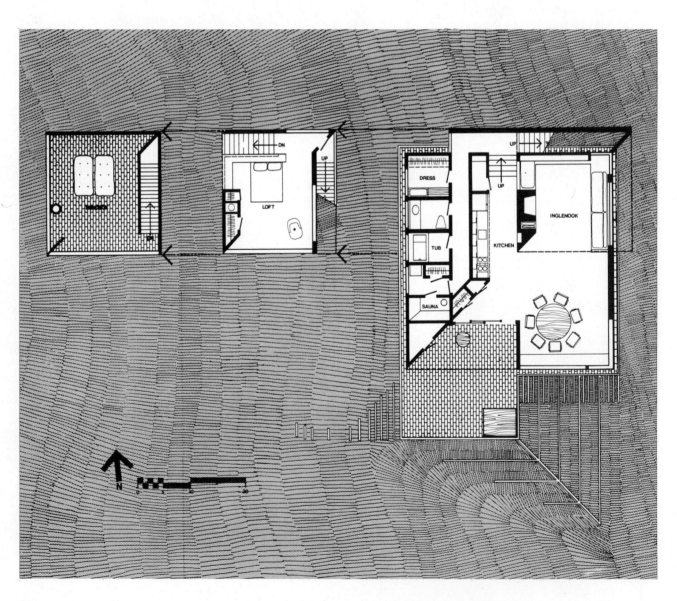

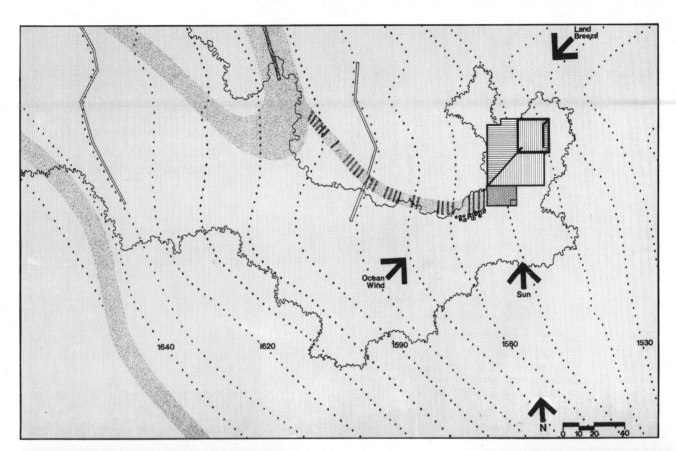

HOUSE CONSTRUCTION SEQUENCE

Homes do not appear magically. They are built according to a logical sequence of building tasks. A conventionally-built house is constructed in this order:

(1) foundation;
(2) framing of walls and roof;
(3) sheathing of walls and roof;
(4) applying roofing;
(5) exterior doors and windows put in;
(6) exterior siding applied.

Each of these steps has to be completed satisfactorily before work can proceed on the next step.

After the "shell" is complete, work can proceed inside the structure despite poor weather. This will cut down on construction time. To finish the interior, the following order is followed:

(1) partitions framed;
(2) rough wiring, plumbing and bathtub installed;
(3) interior door frames put in;
(4) wall and ceiling material applied;
(5) electrical and plumbing work finished;
(6) kitchen cabinets installed;
(7) interior and exterior painted.

Several of the latter steps can take place at the same time.

The time that will elapse for all these steps will depend on several factors, some of which you can control and many of which you can't. Winter can be a good time to schedule construction, for example, because that's when contractors and workers are most likely to be in a "slack" season, and therefore, more readily available for you. On the other hand, severe storms can block access to your site, freeze equipment, and cause delays in deliveries of materials.

Sometimes, shortages of materials can crop up regardless of weather. During the winter of 1973-1974, when "energy crisis" became a standard part of our vocabulary, insulation became very hard to come by and that's been true to a lesser extent during winters ever since. Since you can't finish the interior without putting in insulation first, delays can stall building progress for weeks, if not months.

The number of workers on a job will also affect the time involved. If you and your brother-in-law are framing the house, it will probably take longer than it would for a builder's crew to do the same. If you are using tradesmen, such as plumbers, electricians or masons, a strike can bring your project to a halt, too.

And remember, if you buy a precut or pre-fab home, it may take just a matter of days for the shell to be completed, but interior work can take as long as for any conventional home.

3
What Type of Home?

SPACE AND DESIGN NEEDS

The style and size vacation home you select will depend on a number of factors. Among these are:

- Geographical location, climate considerations.

- Availability of materials in your area of the country.

- Projected use of the home: one season, two seasons, or all-year long.

- Style of life, individual preferences.

- Budget.

This chapter will give you an overview of what types of homes can be built, what types of materials are suitable for different environments, and what types of construction are most economical. But first, let's start by figuring out your space and design needs.

Your space requirements will depend, above all, on the number of people using the home and the activities for which you will use it. Some people just need a small "escape hatch" in the country; others enjoy entertaining lavishly. Honestly evaluate your own preferences before planning your dream house.

If you are single, or if you have no children, you can build a functional plan that includes a bedroom, on one level, of about 500 square feet. Even smaller cabins are, of course, possible.

If your tastes are not that spartan, or if you are planning to entertain or accommodate several guests regularly, you might want to consider a two-level plan that includes about 600 square feet on the first level, and about 200 square feet of storage/sleeping/den space on the second level.

Loft sleeping spaces are particularly dramatic. You get a wonderful sense of spaciousness, looking down to the living area, and a connection to the outdoors not possible in an enclosed bedroom. These types of sleeping areas are not ideal, however, if there are children around; the openness of the space means that noises will carry throughout the house.

If you do have children, figure on about an extra 80- to 100 square feet for every extra bedroom. It may not be necessary to add an additional bedroom for each child; if they are the same sex, they can probably share sleeping accommodations. Teenagers, as we all know, quickly become independent, and may not even want to use the home regularly. An extra bedroom that goes largely unused is very costly in a leisure home.

One guiding principle stands out when trying to determine your space requirements: Less is Better. You should be more concerned about creating a functional, pleasant environment than building a testament to creative architectural thought. You can vacation happily in smaller quarters than you can live in your primary residence. Anything less than a 25 feet x 13 feet living room may give you claustrophobia in the city, but you would be amazed at how that feeling disappears in a much smaller room that looks out to a beach, trees, lake, or mountain!

Appliances such as dishwashers, garbage disposals and compact trashmashers, for example, add an extra expense and drain energy in a second home. In bathrooms, curb your appetite for luxury. Plan instead on arranging the room so that all of the fixtures are on one wall, since this is most economical. Minimum space for one-person bathrooms would be five feet x seven feet two inches. A family's needs could be accommodated in a bathroom of 5 feet x 8 feet, 5 feet 6 inches x 7 feet 4 inches or 5 feet 6 inches x 7 feet 8 inches. (See Chapter 3 for more guidelines on room sizes.)

If you absolutely must have a clothes washer and dryer, consider a combination stackable unit. It will take up less floor space. If the home is to be built in a perenially warm climate, washers and dryers can be located in the carport or garage.

Wind and salt air can wreak havoc with beach houses. Among solutions designed by architect Richard Dodson for this Santa Monica beach house are plexiglass protection for deck area; redwood siding that can weather, needs no painting. Plywood can be stained too. (Courtesy of the California Redwood Association)

Although you are urged to "think small and economical" when it comes to most building and design questions, don't stint in quality on the "guts" of the house: electric wiring, plumbing fixtures and fittings, furnaces, pumps or lumber.

CLIMATE

When it comes to determining what type of heating and air conditioning requirements for your house, again keep in mind its potential use and the climate. Do you really need heat in a home that you won't be using in the winter—or air conditioning in a home shaded by trees or cooled by sea breezes? A house intended for year-round use, of course, will need a more elaborate system than would a one- or two-season cottage.

Let's take a look at how climate will affect the design and materials used. As examples, we'll focus on homes for three popular—and very diverse—types of areas: beach, ski country, and desert.

BEACH HOMES

Beach homes must be built to withstand the considerable beating they will take from the wind, salt, intense sun, and ocean spray over the years.

More and more municipalities are preventing new construction from being built directly on the oceanfront, for many good reasons. The beach environment is particularly vulnerable; tides naturally erode beachfront, while dunes naturally shift and get overgrown. Jetties impede this natural process by helping to keep an existing beach in place.

Severe rainstorms, ice storms and hurricanes have a devastating effect on beachfront properties; many stunning and expensive homes have literally been washed away or crushed. Homeowners' insurance policies, or in some cases, Federal funds for disaster areas, can help people rebuild their properties, but there are few experiences more heart-wrenching than looking over a devastated area and finding your home destroyed.

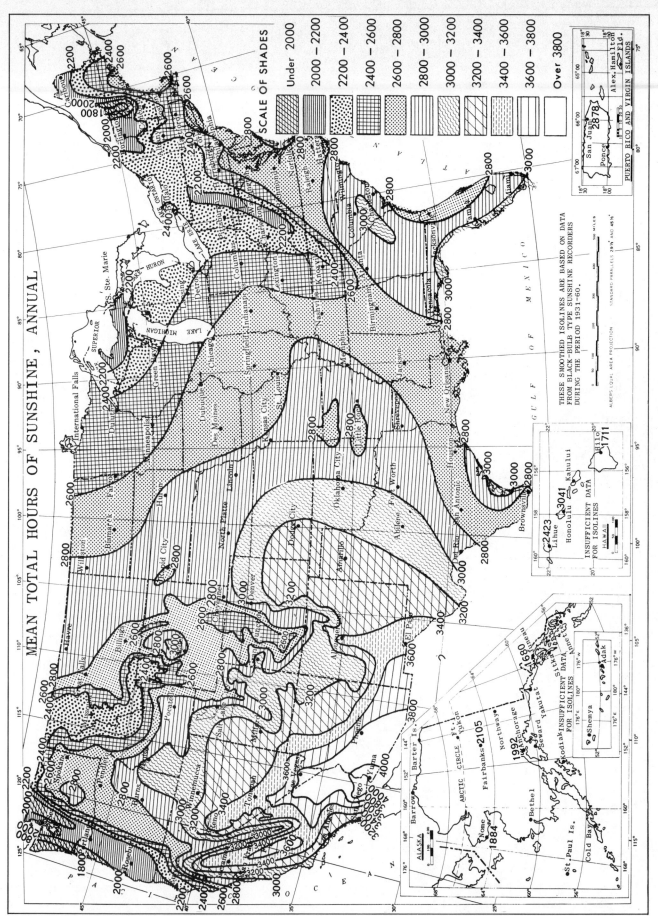

Climate will have a tremendous impact on the design and materials that go into a vacation home. Before you buy property, check records on sunshine, temperature, winds, precipitation for your state. These are available from U.S. Dept. of Commerce, Weather Bureau. Shown here are three representative national maps, depicting Mean Total Hours of Sunshine, Annual; Mean Annual Number of Clear Days; and Mean Annual Temperature Range.

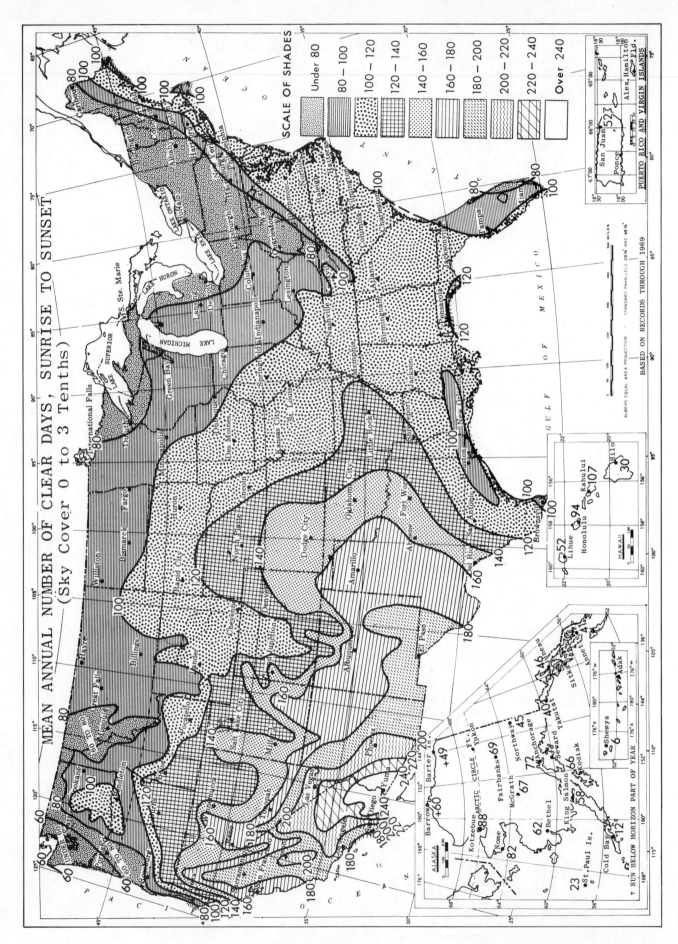

MEAN ANNUAL NUMBER OF CLEAR DAYS, SUNRISE TO SUNSET
(Sky Cover 0 to 3 Tenths)

SCALE OF SHADES

Under 80
80 – 100
100 – 120
120 – 140
140 – 160
160 – 180
180 – 200
200 – 220
220 – 240
Over 240

PUERTO RICO AND VIRGIN ISLANDS

HAWAII

ALASKA

+ SUN BELOW HORIZON PART OF YEAR

ALBERS EQUAL AREA PROJECTION – STANDARD PARALLELS 29½° AND 45½°

BASED ON RECORDS THROUGH 1969

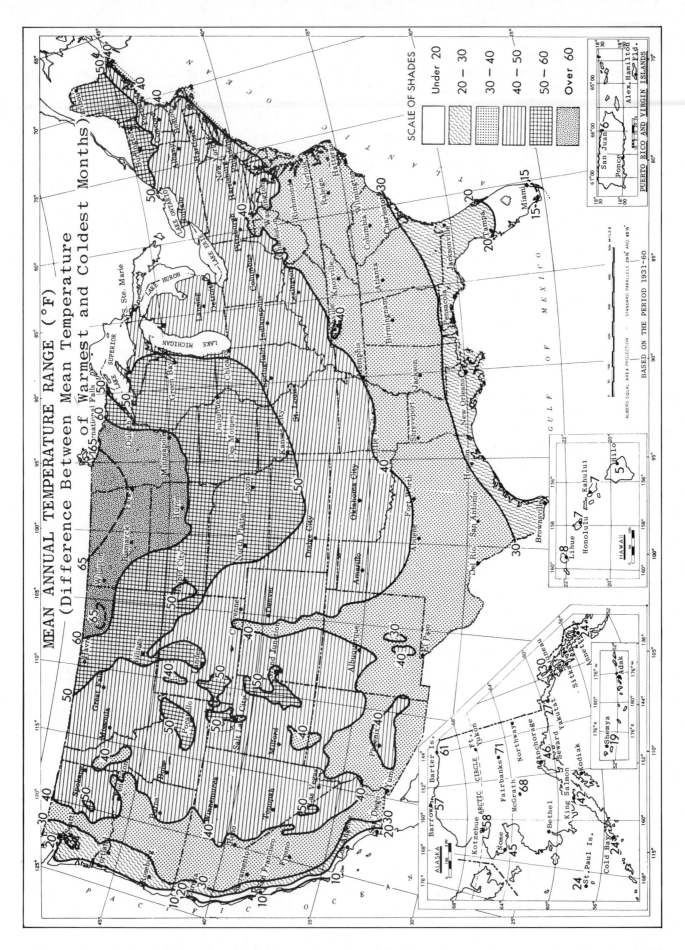

MEAN ANNUAL TEMPERATURE RANGE (°F)
(Difference Between Mean Temperature of Warmest and Coldest Months)

SCALE OF SHADES

Under 20 | 20 – 30 | 30 – 40 | 40 – 50 | 50 – 60 | Over 60

PUERTO RICO AND VIRGIN ISLANDS
Alex. Hamilton Fld.

ALBERS EQUAL AREA PROJECTION — STANDARD PARALLELS 29½° AND 45½°

BASED ON THE PERIOD 1931-60

HAWAII

ALASKA

27

A beach house, then, should be set high enough on piers to allow high tides to come in without distrubing it; or set back far enough to allow a wonderful view over the dunes, protected from the elements.

To minimize the effects of salty air, be sure that the home uses metal supports, metal fasteners and nails that have been galvanized or treated for corrosion and rust-resistance. For exteriors, if wood siding is used, it should be stained, not painted. The paint will only peel or chip. Stained siding weathers far better, and improves with aging. Concrete and stucco are also good materials to use in this type of environment.

Beaches can be very windy. Decks should therefore be situated so that they are not directly in the path of prevailing winds. Awnings, vents, louvers, shutters and outdoor furniture should be secure enough to withstand strong winds.

To prevent the sun from wreaking havoc with furniture and fabrics, use tinted glass or interior shades to block off hot rays. The home should be situated on the site so that the bulk of the window areas will not be facing sunlight directly. And, although it may seem strange to consider heating a home that gets most of its use in the warmth of summer, remember that coastal areas can be damp. A fireplace or heater can help dry out the atmosphere inside.

SKI COUNTRY

If the sea, salt, sun and wind are the bane of a beach home's existence, then heavy snow is the equivalent for a home in ski country.

Unlike beach homes, homes in ski country should be situated so that much of their roof area faces the sun in winter. This will make the interior warmer during those cold weekends. And, situating the house into the wind makes sense because there will be less likelihood of uneven snow buildup during snow storms. Heavy snow swept to one side of the roof can cause structural problems due to too much weight. This is one reason A-frames are so popular in ski resort areas: their steep sides shed snow more easily than more conventional roof designs. Other roof designs that have been used in ski cottages are flat roofs (good for supporting heavy snow loads, but not so good in preventing leakage and providing optimum insulation); no-eave roofs where outside walls are canted and indoor heat warms the roof edge to help melt the snow; and "cold roofs" (two roofs with ventilated air space between them) where the outer roof stays at a like temperature as the snow load. This latter is a very expensive alternative.

Homes in ski country must be designed to withstand heavy snow loads, without allowing wind to "drift" snow unevenly. Flat roofs are good for handling heavy loads. They may have problems with insulation and leaking, however. (Courtesy of Libbey-Owens-Ford Company)

Snow buildup on the sides of the home (from heavy storms, or from falling from the roof) can also be a problem. Snow can cover the main access to the home, so having another "door" at the second level, or building the home 10 feet off the ground, should be considered.

Access to the ski house after a snowstorm can be a problem, too. Garages located off the nearest road that is frequently plowed are an alternative, coupled with foot paths from there to the home.

Frozen pipes can be disastrous in a ski house. To prevent this, water pipes should be located below the frost line, allowing the snow to act as an insulator. Plumbing vents should be high enough so that the snow won't cover them even after a big storm. Pipes should be placed within interior walls or enclosed. (See Chapter 7 for more hints on heating and insulation.)

Like beach houses, ski houses whose exterior is wood should not be painted. The wood should be stained, and allowed to weather.

DESERT HOMES

In the hot, dry climate of the Southwest, staying cool is one of the prime requisites in choosing building design and materials. Materials that will retain the evening's coolness and inhibit heat buildup during the day are concrete, stucco and masonry.

Desert homes should be situated on their sites to limit the expanse of windows facing west, because that side of the house will become uncomfortably hot during the day.

Dramatic overhangs, balconies and porches can act as sunshades, which will keep you cooler during the day. Screened sliding doors can be used to separate a living area from the outside and, left open, can help circulate breezes.

Proper ventilation is essential in these types of homes; floor level vents can help circulate air in otherwise stuffy rooms. Vents should be located at a high point along the roof, since hot air rises. Ceiling fans, besides reminding you of *Casablanca,* can also prove to be effective means of circulating air.

ECONOMICAL DESIGNS AND MATERIALS

Even within the constraints of climate and personal style preferences, there is considerable latitude in picking building materials for a vacation home. These are most economical:

- Two-story homes are generally less expensive to build per square foot than single-story homes, mainly because less roof and foundation areas are needed to cover a like amount of living area. If you are building the home yourself, though, two-story homes offer far more intriguing accident possibilities for you and your helpers!

In hot climates, keeping cool can be helped stressing indoor/outdoor living. As shown, breakfast area in this tropical vacation home runs along one side of glass-walled living room, is shady and sheltered. Also shown is gazebo with horizontal slatted walls, connected to main house by planked bridge. Gazebo is outdoor room, expands space of house. (Courtesy Champion Building Products.)

- Rectangular floor plans cost less per square foot to build than irregular floor plans, including L-shaped or U-shaped.

- Simple gable roofs are most economical. Ridges and valleys increase the roof's cost. Flat and shed roofs are less expensive but have poor drainage and high maintenance cost.

- Basements can provide extra living space if they are dry, well ventilated, and well lighted; the same holds for attics.

- Slab-on-grade construction is cheaper than crawl-space construction. But locating utilities equipment in the main level in the slab-on-grade built home will take away precious living space.

- Walls made of materials that form both exterior and interior wall surface like concrete block walls are more economical than composite walls.

- Hardware floors are cost-effective over a period of time, despite their high initial cost.

- Thick tile flooring costs more than the thinner, but lasts longer. It may be more economical in high-use areas. Vinyl asbestos and sheet vinyl floor coverings can also be used.

- Plywood is the least expensive siding available, and can be stained. Cedar shingles, cedar clapboard, aluminum and vinyl siding are progressively higher-priced, crowned by redwood. (Check local lumber mills if you are in the Southeast, Northeast and Northwest for availability of lumber. It may be less expensive than that available at local lumber yards.)

- Asphalt shingles make inexpensive roofing.

- For window frames, aluminum is less expensive than wood, although wood may be more esthetically pleasing in your home design.

- Consider factory-hung doors for rooms that do not need extra soundproofing. Hollow-core metal doors are least expensive. Solid-core doors can be used for bathrooms.

- Leaving framing materials like roof rafters exposed gives the home a wonderfully rustic look and is more economical than covering it up.

- Finally, fiberglass baths and shower stalls are less expensive than standard units. But check your local building code to make sure they're allowed.

Materials like redwood, marble, slate, masonry and stone can be exquisitely beautiful in a vacation home. They can also be expensive, and require real craftsmanship in installation. If you have the proverbial "champagne tastes and beer budget," do not plan on using these materials extensively in your home.

HOME STYLES

Once you have decided what your space needs and budget would be, you can then consider what kind of configuration appeals to you most to provide that space.

Myriad design possibilities exist: from the simplest one-room cabin of under 200 square feet which you can build yourself (see Chapter 4), to A-frames, traditional Cape Cods, ultra-contemporary wood or masonry fantasies, to log cabins (see Chapter 5), geodesic domes and barns (newly built or recycled).

CABINS: The Original "No-Frills" Home

If you are planning to spend much of your leisure time by yourself, or with one person, or outdoors, the basic one-room cabin may be your most economical and desirable choice.

In all home designs, good traffic patterns are essential. In the one-room cabin, this is even more crucial. A good rectangular design would have essential kitchen appliances, including a small sink, stove and refrigerator, along one wall. A fireplace could be placed in a corner. "Space stretchers" such as a loft sleeping area, built-in window seating or platforms that serve equally well as sitting or sleeping spaces (see Chapter 9) will make the interior that much more workable. A patio off the entrance will complement the indoor/outdoor style of life, while skylights and clerestory windows will bring in natural light and a sense of spaciousness. Another economical touch, which also enhances the rustic feeling, is leaving interior wood studding and rafters exposed.

You should be able to build the basic "no-frills" cabin for under $6,000.

BARNS: The Farm Heritage

Several years ago, buying old barns and "recycling" them for use as primary or second homes, became tremendously popular. The appeal of barns stemmed from their simple, sturdy construction and vast interior spaces filled with stunning layout possibilities. Moreover, many barns were available on large tracts of land that had outlived their use as farm properties.

It's getting tougher and tougher to find old barns to renovate. It's also harder, to locate sources for old barn materials: shingles, hand-hewn beams, end-grain wood blocks, old clapboards and barn boards. Rather than seek out an old barn, then, many people have subsequently chosen "instant" barns, either stick-built or packaged to give them a taste of rustic life.

Construction costs are comparable to, if not higher than, other housing configurations. Key elements are lofts, exposed-beam ceilings, cross-bracing, and rough-textured wood exteriors and interiors. They can be built as small as 1,200 square feet.

Barns may not be suitable for a ski cottage or a beach retreat, but could be an excellent design solution for a country meadow site.

GEODESIC DOMES: Futuristic View

Geodesic domes offer an interesting and unusual design alternative for vacation homes. Although lenders and building inspectors are still skeptical about dome homes, in many parts of the country they have proven to be a sturdy and satisfying form of shelter.

Essentially, a geodesic dome uses triangular space frames to form a spherical structure. Although the home itself appears "round," it uses no curved surfaces in construction. The frames are generally fabricated in a factory, and can be bolted together at the building site.

Although dome homes seem to herald a 21st century vision of housing, with their unusual shapes and factory fabrication, in reality much of the construction is quite conventional.

In roofing, for example, normal building products such as red cedar shingles or redwood shakes or asphalt composition shingles can be applied. For insulation, materials applicable in any wood frame building can be used: glass wool blankets, rock wool, urea-formaldehyde, styrofoam or urethane. The same holds true for plumbing, electrical wiring, kitchens and interior wall surfacing.

Some heating systems that have been used in dome homes include baseboard systems, radiant heat in the slab, pre-fabricated fireplaces, panel-ray heaters, floor furnaces, forced air systems and even solar systems.

Dome shells can be put together by four or five workers over a weekend, and construction tools needed are rudimentary: no cranes, hoists or gin poles are required. The shell price is roughly one-third of the price of the finished home.

There are several advantages to the dome shape for interior design, and if it suits your style of life, this type of house could complement a wooded, hilltop, beach or mountain environment.

There are no columns, beams, trusses or girders to obstruct the interiors, which means great flexibility in interior layouts. Interior partitions need not extend all the way to the dome surface, and can be fabricated so that they can be moved around or removed totally. As a result, the dome-dweller has a great sense of spaciousness on the interior, enhanced by the play of natural light through skylights or windows.

Of course, there are disadvantages to dome homes, too. Some dome dwellers have found furniture arrangement tricky, while others bemoan the lack of vertical walls. And, despite the fact that most domes available do comply with the provisions of the Uniform Building Code, you must make absolutely certain that a chosen package will meet the requirements of a local community before you build.

CUSTOM HOMES: Indulge Your Whims

Custom-designed and built vacation homes are fewer in number than modest cabins, cottages, A-frames and other home styles built conventionally or from packages. You only *think* they're more plentiful because they're the homes celebrated widely in the pages of slick shelter magazines and newspapers. Unquestionably, a home that is designed specifically to suit your needs and habits can not only be visually outstanding, but can also provide the kind of built-in amenities you've always dreamed about.

There is really no limit to the kinds of design wonders that can go into custom homes: cooking centers; hobby displays; built-in movie screens or TV sets that appear and disappear with the touch of a button; or wet bars off the master bedroom so that you don't have to trek to the kitchen for a midnight snack.

Custom homes, of course, are the most expensive to build. Any time you deviate from standard sizes of materials and fixtures, or require many cuts in wood framing members to accommodate unusual layouts, or choose materials like quarry tile for flooring or redwood for siding and decking, construction costs escalate.

If you want a home custom designed and built to suit your individual tastes, you must first seek out an architect with whom you feel compatible. The architect will want to spend time talking with you and your family to get a feeling for the way you live and what you're looking for. He or she will also want to become very familiar with your site.

The architect can be very helpful in locating a mortgage lending source, a builder, and material supply outlets you may not be familiar with yourself. He or she can also watch construction progress on your house to make sure that it is really being built to specifications.

What will all this cost you? Generally, an architect's fee is 15 percent of the cost of building the house, excluding land. Assuming, then, a construction cost of $35 per square foot, having a 1,500 square foot home built would cost $52,500. The architect would get $7,875 on top of that. He would probably also want to charge you on an hourly basis for the time spent in initial consultation.

The fee would be payable in installments: 25 percent when you accept a rough sketch, half when the work begins, and the remainder when you are ready to move in.

HOME "PACKAGES": What to Ask For

There is a home "package" for every popular housing style: simple cabins, A-Frames, Cape Cods, multi-level homes, plus unusual styles like geodesic domes and hexagons. Many packages can be customized, added onto, or put together like building blocks to create a unique look.

Here are a few key questions to ask any package dealer or manufacturer. The answers should go a long way toward giving you the ability and confidence to make an informed judgment about which direction to choose.

- How complete is the package? What materials are included in the package? Some manufacturers' home packages only include exterior walls and roof truss system, while excluding interior walls and roof decking.

- What is the quality of the materials used in the pre-cut home? Are these materials suitable to the climate in your chosen area?

- What is the estimated delivery time once the order has been placed?

- How far must the package be shipped? How much does this add to the cost of the home?

- How long will it take to build the house? How easy is it to erect: does it require much technical construction knowledge? How much labor is actually involved?

- What services are available prior to as well as after the sale? Is help available in obtaining financing? In construction supervision during erection of the home?

- How long has the company been in business? What kind of reputation does it enjoy with past buyers?

- How tightly constructed is the home when finished? Is it energy efficient? Can it be expanded or changed to accommodate alternate energy sources?

(See Chapter 6 for more details on pre-cut, prefabricated and modular homes.)

STOCK PLANS: Try Before You Buy

If you don't want to go to the expense of hiring an architect and having a home custom-built, but don't want to restrict yourself to manufactured homes either, there is another alternative: buying stock home plans and having a builder cost it out and construct it for you.

Several firms specialize in providing home plans (see chapter 10). These include blueprints, materials lists and specification outlines. To select a home that seems most suitable, go through the suppliers' catalogues, which can be ordered for several dollars apiece. These catalogues usually provide floor plans, artists' renderings and a brief description of the house. There are literally hundreds of plans available for vacation homes: chalets, A-frames, round houses, octagonal, traditional cottages, log cabins and multi-levels.

If they serve no other purpose, these catalogues can sharpen the focus on your own taste in housing styles!

The plans themselves cost upwards of $50 apiece. The benefit of using stock plans for small, simple homes which you may want to build yourself is that the plans are already worked out for you. This will help you with your banker, your subcontractor and your building-mates.

Breathtaking views of the ocean from house and deck make this George Klett designed dwelling a year-round retreat. (Courtesy of Karl Riek)

Whether renovated or newly constructed, a spacious barn makes an ideal vacation retreat for that individual or family who needs lots of inner space. This barn was renovated to the design of William Weber Kirsch and is in the heart of Napa County, CA. (Photo by Karl Riek)

Architect Edward A. Cuetara, AIA, captures light and space with this Martha's Vineyard, MA. vacation home. (Photo by Michael Zide)

Many design possibilities are available from manufactured housing producers. This contemporary with a "crow's nest" is indicative of what's available today. (Courtesy of Acorn Structures)

When the budget permits, solar heating and hot water systems are a nice addition to a leisure home. (Photo courtesy of Acorn Structures)

Small, compact and easily constructed are the virtues of this lakeside home. L-shaped deck is situated to take in both land and lake views. (Photo courtesy of Jim Walter Homes).

Natural wood siding and judicious placement of windows make this weekend retreat a lovely sight to behold from both inside and out. (Photo courtesy of Acorn Structures)

4
Preliminary Steps

HANDLING SITE IMPROVEMENTS

As we pointed out in Chapter 1, you should not purchase any tract of land unless you are satisfied that basic needs such as water, sewage disposal, and electricity can be reasonably accommodated. And, just as this type of verification represents the "first step" toward your land purchase, bringing in those utilities represents the "first step" in home construction.

ROAD BUILDING

How accessible is your property? Naturally, one of the prime considerations in building a vacation home is "to get away from it all"; you don't want to be so near a major thoroughfare that the noise and exhaust will disturb your serenity. One of the possible implications of buying property far from the beaten path, however, is that you will have to build a road to get to your home site.

Before you do that, make sure that you have the legal right to cross other's property to get to your own. Chances are, the party selling the property to you already has that right. But if it's just a verbal agreement between neighbors, you would be well advised to have it set down in writing, preferably in the contract of sale.

If a road already exists, you should set the easement right at 60 feet in width. That way, if a new road has to be built to replace the existing one, you will still have some protection.

If a road does not exist, that will be the first building priority. Without it, no one will be able to deliver building materials. Costs for building a road depend on the length of the route, the type of materials used, and the condition of the terrain. Contacting a road contractor to get an estimate of what it would cost to build the road would be wise before you buy the property.

A "minimum" dirt road, over flat, clear terrain,

would cost more than $2 a running foot to build. A blacktop road under the same conditions would be about three times the cost of a dirt road. And, if shrubbery, trees, or boulders have to be removed, or considerable grading work has to be done, the cost is higher still.

In the course of building a road or driveway, particularly if you are cutting into hilly terrain, it may be necessary to hold the earth that has been moved by means of a retaining wall. Cinder blocks represent the most economical method of creating a wall, although they may not be as esthetically pleasing as, say, railroad ties. A retaining wall of railroad ties can cost several thousands of dollars or more, depending on the length of the wall and the number of ties needed.

BRINGING IN UTILITIES: Water

Your property must have a year-round source of water that is sufficient to meet your needs. Minimum requirement for home use is about fifty gallons per day per person.

There are a number of sources of water supply: some public utility companies provide water, while others have public water districts or private water companies you can hook into.

If your property has a lake, pond, or stream, these may also prove to be sources of water for your home. To find out whether or not they are safe, check your county health department, the local Farm Advisor or U.S. Geological Survey.

You might also want to check with the Water Resources Department in your state to find out whether or not there are any plans for building dams on rivers nearby, which might affect your property. And, the Fish and Game Code in your state will let you know how your stream is classified. Violation of classifications can result in heavy penalties. One such violation is fishing in spawning areas.

If the water on your property is usable, you'll need a shallow pump, piping, and a foot valve that fits onto the end of the line, to tap into it. This kind of system does have its drawbacks. It is difficult to design the system to ensure that it will work in the winter, when the water might freeze. Problems arise, too, during long dry spells. Contamination can occur, too, if a neighboring home has sewage difficulties.

If you can't tap into a water supply through a utility company or nearby lake, pond or stream, you will have to have a well dug on your property.

About 90 percent of all water beneath the ground's surface occurs in the top 200 feet, but the average depth of all domestic water wells in the U.S. is less than 50 feet. Again, the State Water Resources Department and local health department will be able to give you a pretty good idea of how deep you'll have to dig before you reach water.

Water is found in three types of formations beneath the ground: in layers of sand, in layers of gravel, and in porous rock or in cracks in a rock.

Finding a possible source of water on an individual tract of land is far from an exact science. The usual procedure for finding a good water vein is to have a well dug. One guideline to keep in mind, of course, is that the well will have to be located at least 50 feet away from septic fields, for health's sake.

When a well driller sets up his rig and starts digging in a possible site, there is no guarantee that he will actually find a water vein on the first try or subsequent tries. But you'll have to pay for the drilling nevertheless. Well drilling costs range from abut $5 to $15 per foot.

Besides having the well drilled, you'll need to have a pump installed, which can cost about $500, plus a water storage tank put into the house, which costs less than the pump. In total, then, creating a working water supply can cost up to $2,000.

BRINGING IN UTILITIES: Electricity

Unless you have a real taste for rudimentary living, you will also have to concern yourself with bringing in electricity to your site.

The cost for doing this will depend on how far your site is from the nearest utility pole. Poles should be placed about every 200 feet across the property, and the cost of each pole and wire varies from $100 to $500 installed.

If you believe that above-ground poles and wires are unsightly, check with the utility company about installing underground wiring. It costs more, but esthetically it enhances your property and will ulti-

mately prove to be a "plus" if you ever decide to sell your home.

Generally, 100 amp service should be sufficient.

HANDLING SEWAGE DISPOSAL

If your vacation home cannot be connected up to a public sewage disposal system, then you will need to install a septic tank sewage disposal system.

Not all types of property can accommodate such systems, however, so before you buy the property, find out what the land's absorption capacity is, and what type of absorption field will be required to handle your needs. Your building department will give you requirements for this.

SOIL PERCOLATION TESTS

Soil is tested for absorption capacity by "percolation" tests. These can be conducted by local health departments, civil engineers or licensed firms in the business. The tests involve boring six or more holes of four to 12 inches in diameter and as deep as the proposed trenches or seepage bed, throughout the proposed absorption field. Sand and gravel are placed on the bottom of these holes.

At least 12 inches of water are poured into each hole, with water added to keep the water level 12 in-

The average depth of all domestic water wells in the U.S. is 50 feet or less beneath the ground's surface. The way to tap water vein is by drilling wells. (Rig shown here courtesy of Deeprock Mfg. Company)

ches above the gravel for at least four hours, preferably overnight. The percolation rate is the drop in water level over a 30-minute period, multiplied by two.

In sandy soil, water seeps more rapidly and the test is run over a shorter period, with the rate calculated during the final 10 minutes of a one-hour period.

SEPTIC SYSTEMS

A septic tank disposal system works this way: the effluent from the tank is carried through draintile to points in the property where it is absorbed and filtered by surrounding soil. The draintile is laid in trenches, which are then covered over with soil.

The rate at which effluent moves into and through the soil is a major factor in determining how well a septic system will work. Soil permeability should be moderate to rapid, and your percolation rate should be at least one inch per hour. But there are other influences, too: ground-water level, soil depth, underlying material, slope, and proximity to streams or lakes.

At least four feet of soil material between the bottom of the trenches or seepage bed and any rock formation is needed for absorption, filtration, and purification of effluent. Deep, permeable soils are desirable.

Flood plains are not suitable for absorption fields; nor are slopes that are more than 15 percent. On more gently sloping lands, trenches can be dug on the contour so that effluent flows slowly through tile or pipe and disperses properly over the absorption field.

Your local public health department will be able to tell you what kind of standards it has set for absorption field sizes. These are generally calculated by the number of bedrooms in the house.

For example, let's assume that you want to build a

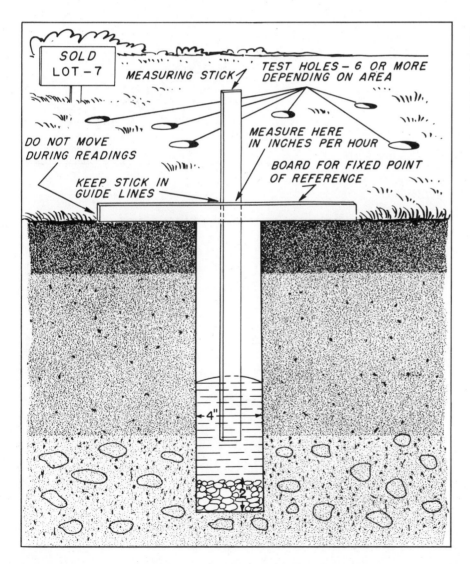

Many test holes, each of four to 12 inches in diameter, must be dug for percolation tests. Tests indicate absorption capacity of soil, important in determining size of absorption field. (Soil Conservation Service, U.S. Dept. of Agriculture.)

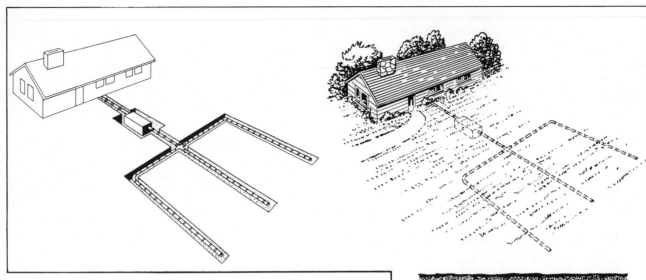

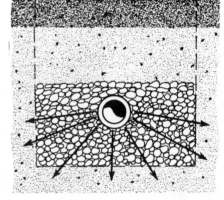

Effluent from septic tank is absorbed and filtered by soil in field after being carried through draintile laid in trenches, as shown here. (Soil Conservation Service, U.S. Dept. of Agriculture.)

Deep, permeable soils are good for septic tank disposal systems, but slopes of more than 15 percent will present a problem. Flood plains are out as possibilities for absorption fields. (Soil Conservation Service, U.S. Dept. of Agriculture.)

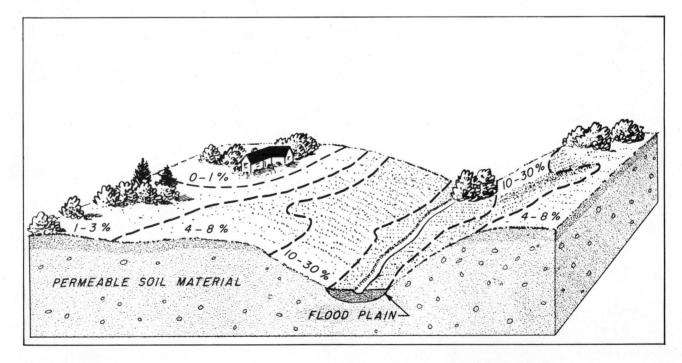

two-bedroom house on land that has a soil percolation rate of two inches per hour. According to the U.S. Department of Health, Education and Welfare, the area required for the absorption field is 250 square feet for each bedroom on property that has a soil percolation rate of two inches per hour. Hence, the absorption area required would be 500 square feet.

To determine the length of trench and tile or pipe required for this house, divide the total area by the trench width, two feet. Trenches should not be longer than 100 feet, nor should they be spaced closer than six to eight feet apart. For this house, an absorption field layout might comprise four trenches of about 62 feet long, or three trenches, each about 84 feet long.

To get the total area, in square feet, to be occupied by the absorption field, multiply the total trench length by the distance between trench and center lines.

You will need a larger absorption field if the soil has a slower absorption rate.

Do not plan on laying an absorption field within 50 feet of a stream or lake, or your source of water, for these can be easily contaminated.

SOIL SURVEYS

A soil survey can give you a reasonably good idea of what type of soil your general area contains. These surveys can point out what the area's soil's limitations are, and how it might be expected to perform as host to an absorption field.

Soil surveys of counties or other areas are published by the Soil Conservation Service of the U.S. Department of Agriculture. In fact, a booklet entitled "List of Published Soil Surveys" available from the Department indicates soil surveys published for all 50 states, plus Washington, D.C. and Puerto Rico. The surveys contain maps as well as general information about the agriculture and climate of the area, plus descriptions of each kind of soil.

You can also get advice and planning aid from the local planning commission, building inspector, health department, engineering or agricultural department of colleges and universities, or State board of health.

Costs for septic system installation can range from about $600 to more than $2000.

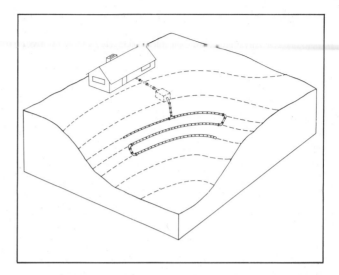

Chart shows size of absorption fields needed for homes. If soil percolation rate is two in. per hour, required absorption area per bedroom is 250 sq. ft. (Soil Conservation Service, U.S. Dept. of Agriculture.)

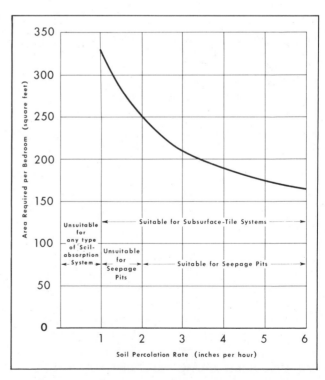

Tile lines are laid on contour on sloping land. This will allow effluent to flow slowly through the tile or pipe. (Soil Conservation Service, U.S. Dept. of Agriculture.)

LAYING OUT THE HOUSE

On one hand, you have a site. On the other, you have your house plan. How do you put the pieces together so that your home will take the most advantage of light, air and view while protecting you from the elements and minimizing heat gain or loss?

The first step is to pinpoint a building site that has firm, well-drained soil. This point cannot be overemphasized. Over the life of your home, water can cause critical damage either insidiously or dramatically. Moisture can eat away at building foundations; flooding can wreak havoc with your septic system and basement.

Visit your property after a rainfall. This will give you a first-hand view of how the site retains water. And, of course, check the local building department, health department, and/or a soils engineer for more technical expertise.

Assuming that your site presents no drainage problems, here are a few guidelines to assist you in finding the best spot to lay out the home:

- Don't build in low places where air might be trapped.

- Location on top of a ridge will expose your house to higher winds, hotter sun and noises from a valley below.

- Valleys are generally cooler and quieter as well as closer to water sources. Sloping sites that are well-drained are very good for basements.

The layout of your house will not only affect your views from different rooms and therefore your leisure time ambience, but will also influence energy use. Here, then, are guidelines for laying out the house to enhance your experience and conserve energy at the same time.

The living room should be oriented to the east or the south to take advantage of the sun for heating.

The dining area can also be oriented to the south or east. If the room is located on the west side of the house, it would be wise to plant deciduous trees or other kinds of shrubbery outside. This will cut down on glare and overheating during the summer. Building a deck off the dining room facing west will also create a pleasant environment.

The kitchen should have an eastern or southern exposure to utilize natural sunlight. A kitchen facing north or west will be darker, chillier in the winter, and therefore considerably less cheerful than a kitchen facing south or east.

Bathrooms can face in any direction; the amount of time spent in the bathroom is relatively short, compared to other parts of the house.

Bedrooms should be placed facing east or south. During the summer, an east- or south-facing bedroom won't become terribly warm until after you've used the room, and by the time you're ready to use it again, it will have cooled off after several hours in the shade. In the winter, the early morning sun will help heat the room. If your bedroom faces west, you may have to install a fan or air conditioning to cool it off before retiring at night.

If any of your major activity areas face north, consider planting evergreens outside. They will act as a windbreak during the winter because they are green and full throughout the year.

PIERS AND FOUNDATIONS

A house can't be plunked down directly on a building site! It must rest on piers or on a foundation for structural strength and protection from the elements. Piers are heavy, vertical support members made of masonry, wood or metal.

And before you dismiss difficult sites such as waterfront properties, beaches, or steep hilly mountain properties as unbuildable, consider the possibility of building a house on piers.

One form of pier building is pole construction, which offers several advantages over more conventional foundations. It is cheaper, it lends itself to many design possibilities and it's less disturbing to the environment.

Cost savings are available using pole construction, and when properly preserved, pole construction will last for 40 years or more, with great resistance to severe weather.

There are two types of pole construction: pole frame and platform.

In pole frame houses, pressure-treated wood poles are the main vertical members. They extend from below the ground surface to the roof. They support the vertical weight of the building as well as provide lateral resistance to flood, wind and earthquake.

One advantage of this method is that once the poles have been set, the roof can be built before the walls are erected, which makes building partitions, walls and floors more convenient in poor weather.

On hillsides, a platform can be used, permitting conventional construction methods to be used on the house.

Before planning pole placement and home design, seek advice from a soils engineer, architect or builder about your site. Factors to be considered are the proposed size of the house, the steepness of the slope,

Steep sites, such as this canyon-side site in San Diego, can accommodate pole homes. Poles can be installed by pile driving, drilling, machine driving or by hand. (Photo courtesy of Stuart MacArthur Resor, Architect.)

Advantage of pole construction (one form of pier building) is that surrounding environment remains relatively undisturbed, as shown in construction of this four-bedroom, mountain-top- tri-level in Del Mar, Calif. (Photo courtesy of Stuart MacArthur Resor, Architect.)

the type of soil and drainage patterns on the site. These will affect the types of poles to be used, how deep they should be placed, and what type of backfilling they'll need.

Poles can be installed by pile driving, drilling, machine driving or, of course, by hand. The latter is cheapest and disturbs the environment least of all methods. On the other hand, it's likely to take longer and prove more of a drain on your physical stamina than you'd bargained for, if you're doing it yourself. If adequate pole embedment is not possible, a keywall of concrete should be connected to the frame, preferably at floor level, to reinforce a pole platform.

It is important to try to preserve natural vegetation and drainage patterns around and under the pole house, to forestall slides and erosion. A slide can occur, for example, if the backfill around the pole settles, causing the area around the pole to soak up water.

Poles can be backfilled with concrete, soil and cement, sand, pea gravel or crushed rock. Least expensive is clean sand. Also economical is a soil and cement combination, which is made by mixing the earth removed from the holes with cement in a five-to-one ratio, then wetted and tamped into place. Particles larger than one inch should be removed from the earth.

One tip from an experienced architect is: when putting poles into a steep site where there is a road on top, place a 2x10 into the holes; slide the pole down the hill, butt first, until it hits the 2x10. Then lift the other end.

To plumb and center the poles, this architect recommends having two people with plumb bobs standing at right angles and 20 feet or so away from the pole. Use 2x10s to pry the bottom of the pole into the

correct position, then start eyeballing it with plumb bobs. Get the bottom 10 feet vertical; the upper portion can be manipulated into the correct position later. Poles can be framed with pairs of beams, girders or rafters: one on each side.

One thing to keep in mind in planning a pole house is that your insulation and mechanical systems must be particularly suited for its use. The underside of the house is exposed, which can make mechanical systems more vulnerable to freezing, moisture and other climatic problems. A few hints are:

- Keep all domestic and drain piping within insulated joist spaces.

- Group piping to drop to grade at one point, back from the perimeter of the structure. An insulated enclosure can protect the drop.

- Put rigid insulation on top of the floor; put another floor covering such as carpeting on top of the insulation.

- Seal undersides of joists, filling the spaces between them with blown material or foil-faced insulation batts.

Precut and prefabricated homes can be placed on platforms, which can also mean some cost savings for you. And, you don't need a difficult, hilly, rocky or sandy site for pier construction. Pier homes can be built on flat land, too, which would give you a "treetop" view of your property as well as more shady outdoor areas to enjoy during hot weather.

If pier construction is not to your liking, however, or it your site is relatively flat and well-drained, then a concrete foundation (either slab-on-grade, or with basement or crawl space) would be more suitable.

It is particularly important for the foundation to be built right; if it's not, your house could settle unevenly, which causes cracks, and nothing in your home will be level.

Before the concrete slab is poured in slab-on-grade construction, all utilities should be placed where they will eventually go. Utilities will be installed before walls and floors are enclosed and finished. Likewise, drains and sewers should be placed before foundation footings are poured.

In crawl space construction, floor joists usually span about half the house's width, with a beam supporting the ends near the center of the house. Smaller joists can be used with shorter spans, with joists supported with two or three beams.

In concrete-slab construction, the thickness of the slab under load-bearing walls can be increased instead of requiring pouring of separate footings.

Consider that chimney or column footings support a heavier load per square foot than sidewall footings. The footings must be sized in proportion to their load; heavy loads require large footings, while lighter loads need smaller footings.

DEALING WITH LOCAL BUILDING DEPARTMENTS

Throughout the entire building process, you will be dealing with local building officials. In fact, before you turn over your first shovelful of soil, you will have gone through a process of seeking a building permit. In many communities, even the most rural, your plans will have to comply with local zoning regulations, or you will have to get a zoning variance.

There are probably as many different types of zoning officials, building department heads and building inspectors as there are types of human personalities. But one thing is certain; you must maintain good communications with you building department and the building inspector. Particularly if your house is atypical of the kind of construction generally found in the area, you will undoubtedly have to participate in protracted discussions with local officials, who may be skeptical about the design's suitability.

As in most social situations, the rules of common sense apply. Be courteous, inquisitive and respectful. Belligerence, anger and aggressiveness won't work. Many zoning and building department officials are quite knowledgeable and helpful. Seek their guidance. They can give you invaluable tips not only about what local regulations permit you to do and prevent you from doing, but they can also give you good insight about availability of materials, past building experience in the area, local labor conditions and more.

Many building departments conduct four inspections during the course of a home's construction. The first encompasses the foundation, prior to laying. The second takes place after the roof is framed and pipes, chimneys and vents have been put in. The third is to inspect the walls before wallboard has been applied or siding has been put up. Finally, when the house is complete and ready for occupancy, the building department will make a last inspection and hopefully issue a certificate of occupancy.

If you decide to purchase a precut or prefabricated home, do not automatically assume that it will meet local building regulations just because the manufacturer says it will. Find out what, if any, modifications will have to be made.

A geodesic dome structure built in the Northeast is a case in point. Approvals for this home took longer than normal because the building department had trouble ascertaining whether or not it would take snow loads of 30 pounds per square foot, a local requirement. Finally, it required that the architect certify that the house would, indeed, take that kind of load. Moreover, they deemed that the exterior of the house was all roof, and required exterior roofing material put on practically from the ground up!

In construction, the phrase "time is money" is paramount. Delays like these will ultimately push up your building costs. If they can be avoided by doing as much "homework" as you can beforehand, the result is more than worth it.

5
Building from Scratch

A small vacation house you build yourself can be a most rewarding experience. But when things go wrong—and they easily can—it becomes an overly long, tiresome and expensive proposition. In this chapter, we'll detail the major steps involved in laying out and building the foundation, the superstructure and details on finishing. By the time you finish reading this chapter, you will have a better understanding of what's involved in home construction and whether or not such a large project is right for you.

Before you go any further in this chapter, ask yourself a few key questions: Do you *really* have the time for such a project? Do you have enough money for materials, and some left over to hire professional help if you need it? Is your interest in the project strong enough to carry you through to completion?

If you've answered "no" to one or more of the above, think about hiring someone to do some or all of it for you. Perhaps hire a contractor to build the foundation and superstructure. Hire subcontractors to do the plumbing, electrical and mechanical and then you finish the inside. There are a variety of ways to tackle such a project; find the method that is right for you. Although hiring someone else to do the major work is not like building the house yourself, at least you will have a nicely finished dwelling.

Further, if you are handy with tools (don't build a house yourself if you're not) but have never built a house before, keep the following in mind: (1) the house will take longer to build than projected; (2) it will cost more than estimated; (3) there will be less time to work on it than anticipated. These are "corollaries" to "Murphy's Law".

Still interested? Then we can proceed with some of the more positive aspects of building a small vacation or leisure house. If you can do the job efficiently and relatively quickly, making few mistakes, project expense will be little more than the cost of materials. If you do not have a great deal of money to put into a second home, this alone could put the project in reach. Also the psychic gratification of undertaking (and completing) the project is great. And finally, in the process of building a small house, you will develop a new skill that has its own rewards.

PLANNING THE HOUSE

Planning a house takes a lot of time and effort and is detailed in other sections of this book. What is detailed here is a very simple house. It's built with a concrete block crawl space; the walls of the unit are constructed of wood studs and plywood siding. The roof is plywood sheathed and finished in an asphalt shingle. Windows, trim and finishing detail are up to you.

Although there are many other types of materials with which you can work, these were selected because they are really the easiest. With siding, for instance, there are a great many other types which can be used. But plywood panels can be nailed to stud walls while the walls are still on the flat and then the walls can be tipped into place. With this complete there is little else to do with the exterior wall but stain it as you see fit.

One final bit of advice before we get into the construction of the unit. If you are going to build it yourself, keep it small and simple. A small, well-finished unit is 1000 percent better than a large, overly ambitious shelter that is never quite finished.

LAYING OUT FOUNDATION

The layout of the foundation is one of the first "physical" steps you undertake in the construction of a house. It is also one of the most important. Two elements are crucial: (1) you must lay out the foundation on the proper location on the site; and (2) you must lay it out *square* and *level*.

Building a small house yourself can be an exciting project. When the project gets too big, it can become overly complicated and costly. Detailed below are the basic elements of a small straightforward dwelling. (Courtesy of American Plywood Association)

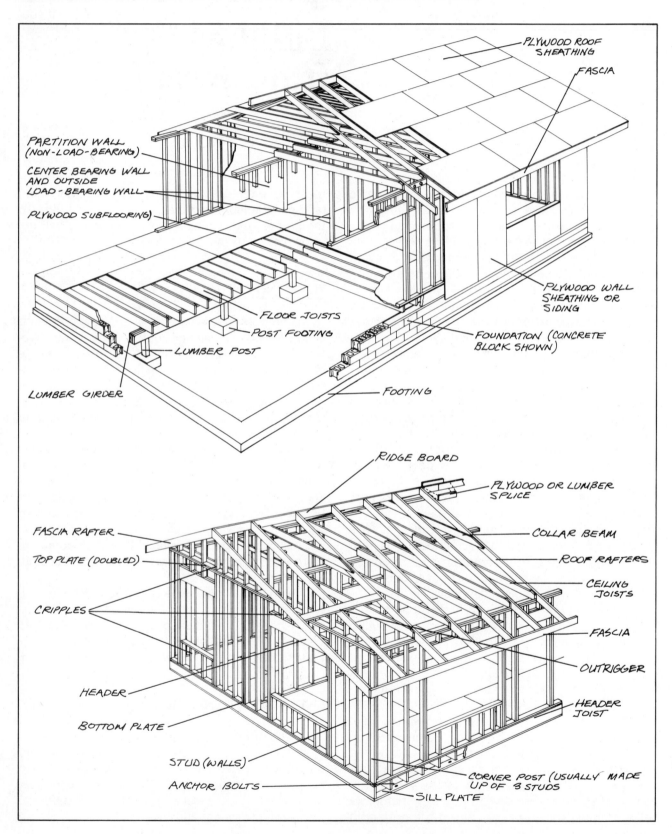

If you think that laying out the foundation on the proper location of the site is obvious, it's not. On small lots, municipalities are very exacting in their requirements. If you have a half-acre vacation lot, the zoning code may specify that the unit be set back 40 feet from the road and either 20 feet or 30 feet from the adjoining property. This can give you very little flexibility. And if you don't adhere to one or more of these requirements, you may have a very difficult time getting a certificate of occupancy. Obviously, this becomes far less important if you have purchased half a mountainside or 10 acres of field upon which to build.

As for the second point, creating a foundation which is square and level, a mistake here in the early stages of construction will come back to haunt you. It will add to the cost of labor and materials if not done correctly.

Once you have taken all zoning requirements into consideration, you need to look at the site from the point of view of drainage, sunlight, grade, trees and view. And then, be cautious. Unless you have seen your property in all four seasons of the year, be suspicious of low-lying areas. It could be a flood plain.

You may build your house in early summer and autumn only to find it under a foot of water in the Spring. A local architect, engineer or building inspector can be invaluable in helping you select a location if you are unsure. If you have a stream running through your property, you're lucky, but make sure you are a substantial distance above water level.

And as mentioned earlier in the book, select a location which will enable you to bring materials right to the house site easily.

Once a site has been selected, clear the immediate area in and around the proposed foundation. You don't have to defoliate the entire property, just clear the foundation area and the space immediately around it. You will need a clear view.

If you can afford it, hire a surveyor to lay out the foundation. He has instruments and the corners of the house will be laid out exactly square and level.

If you can't afford it, here's how to do it yourself. As in Illustration 1 locate each outside corner of the house and drive in a 2x2 stake. Drive them deeply so they will not pull or be knocked out. Then drive small nails into the top of the stakes to indicate the outside

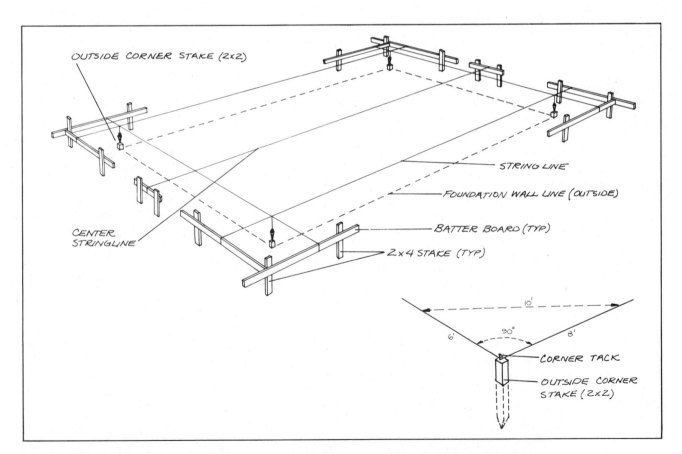

1. Foundation must be laid out exactly square. This shows you a typical layout. If possible, hire a surveyer or architect to get you started on the right foot. (Courtesy of American Plywood Association)

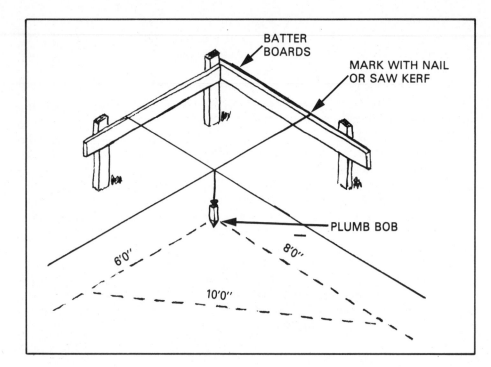

2. Squaring corners by the rule of 3, 4, 5.

line of the foundation wall (not footings). Now check for square.

Measure the diagonals, corner to corner to see if they are equal. A rectangle will always have equal diagonals if all corners are in square. To check each corner, use the 3, 4, 5 triangle concept. That is, if a right triangle has one side which is three feet and another which has four feet, the hypotenuse will be five feet. You can use multiples of this concept. To check corners, measure down six feet on one side, eight feet on the other and if in square, the hypotenuse will be 10 feet.

Once corners of the foundation are located and exactly square, drive in three more stakes per corner at least three or four feet outside the perimeter. Don't place them any closer than this or they'll get in the way or become dislodged.

Then as in Illustration 2, nail in 1x6 batter boards horizontally so that top edges are all level with one another. Then tie a string across the tops of opposite batter boards. Using a plumb bob, adjust strings so that the plumb bob just touches the tack which represents the corner of the foundation. Then cut "saw kerfs" or notches where the string touches the batter boards. This is done so that once string has been removed, you can later retie the string without having to measure it all again.

Next, locate the girder location, which will usually run down the centerline of the house. Check your house plans to determine the exact location. On very small cabins you might not need a center girder.

Once you find the girder location, install more batter boards, as in Illustration 3.

Once everything is set up, you must again check for level. Again, a surveyor can handle this quite easily and more quickly than you can. If you want to do it yourself, the best way is to secure a very straight piece of lumber between 10 feet and 14 feet long. You will use this as a giant ruler or straightedge.

Using the straightedge in conjunction with a good carpenter's level, you will drive stakes around the perimeter of the house. Resting one end of the straightedge on a batter board, drive in the first stake, at a point on the foundation line which does not exceed the distance of the straightedge.

Hammer it in. With the straightedge resting on the batter board and on the newly driven stake, check for level by placing the carpenter's level on the horizontal board. If not level, adjust the newly driven stake until it is. Next, hammer in a second stake further down the foundation line; again, the distance should not exceed the length of your straightedge.

Now place the straightedge on the first and second stake. Adjust the second stake for level. Continue this process of driving stakes and leveling until you get to the end of the foundation line. With the last stake driven, check for level by placing straightedge on the last stake and the batter boards nearest to you.

Continue driving stakes and adjusting for level all around the foundation line. Your final check will come when you drive in the final stake, which should be near first stake driven. Check these for level. If they are level, then all your batter boards are level. But once again, the most efficient way to accomplish this is using a surveyor's level.

Once excavation gets under way, the corner stakes which denote the foundation corners and the temporary stakes you drove will be removed. Therefore, it is extremely important that the batter boards and string lines be exactly level. Later, when the excavation is checked, the strings will be retied in the saw kerfs.

FOOTINGS AND FOUNDATION

The next step is to dig the footing trenches. This can be done by hand or by machine. Although a machine costs money, you should spend the money, if your labor and time are worth anything at all. Doing it by hand is hard, dirty and tiring work.

Concrete footings are usually preferred. Properly sized and constructed, they prevent the house from settling—which in turn prevents cracks in the walls. Although your building code will determine what type of footing must be used, typically footings are located about one foot below frost line in "undisturbed earth." Footings cannot be placed on top soil or on any type of loose soil because this will not support the tremendous weight of the house.

Footings can be dug in one of two ways. You can dig a relatively small trench and then use the earth walls as your "form." Or you can dig a relatively wide trench and then install wooden forms in which to pour the concrete.

If you want to use wooden forms, dig a trench to the specified depth, making it wide enough for you to climb in there and install the forms. The exact width won't affect anything, but the depth will. If you have a frost line of two feet in your area, dig the footing trench three feet deep (if you want a one-foot footing). If you dig deeper than you intended, you will have to fill the gap with concrete, not loose earth.

Once the trench has been dug, rehang the strings on the batter boards and, using the plumb bobs, locate the corners of the foundation-to-be. When you start to lay the concrete blocks, they will have to sit in the center of the footing. Remember, the footing is wider than the foundation block. Therefore, when you determine the actual corner, you will have to measure out a few more inches to locate the footing line.

Here's an example: Let's say you are using 10-inch concrete block for your foundation wall, and your footings will be 18 inches wide. Once you determine the corner of that foundation wall, the footing will extend another four inches on either side of the founda-

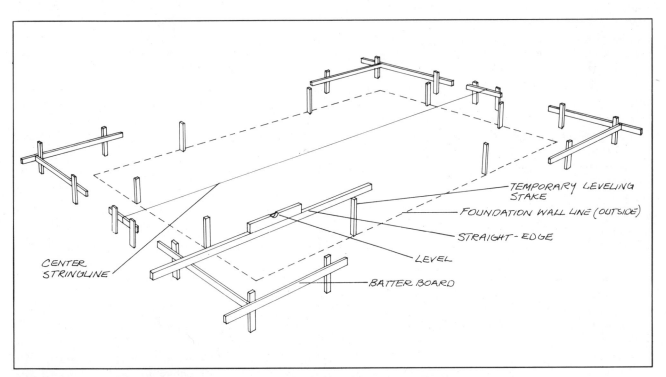

3. Once a basic layout is completed, centerline girder location should be established. When all is ready, hammer in temporary stakes and check carefully for level. (Courtesy of American Plywood Association)

tion wall. Thus, if you had your footing in place, and centered the block, you would see—looking straight down on it—four inches of footing on the outside, the 10-inch block, and four inches of footing on the inside as in Illustration 4.

The footing must be outlined on both sides of the foundation wall. You can do this with a string or you can do it with a powdered chalk. The footing forms can be made of either lumber or plywood. Usually, the material used is such a mess by the time you finish the footings that it must all be thrown away. So select a sturdy but inexpensive material.

If you use plywood, you can cut a 4x8 sheet into one-foot widths and, using stakes, install it in the trench. Although you can get a fairly exact footing by this method, you will have to spend more in both time and materials setting the whole thing up. If possible, try to get the original trenches dug narrowly enough so that you can use the earth as a form. But remember, that trench has to be exact.

With the trenches and forms ready, you can now dig the footings for the supports which will hold the centerline girder in place. These holes are called post footings and are between 20 inches and 24 inches square (check codes and plans). Usually, it is easier to build box forms for this pouring rather than use earth walls as a form. Boxes for these post footings can be made similarly to the above mentioned forms.

When forms are all ready, check your plans to see if you have to install steel reinforcing bars. Many codes demand them; they will tie the entire footing together.

When ordering the concrete, estimate carefully how much you will need. It is better to err on the side of too much rather than too little. Concrete is ordered in cubic yards. One cubic yard contains 27 cubic feet of concrete. If you were to pour a footing which is one foot deep by one foot wide, you would get 27 running feet of footing from a yard. You can figure out how much concrete you need by calculating the dimensions of your footing. If, however, you are using earth sidewalls as a form, order a few more yards because the excavation will never be exact.

For concrete, have extra help at the building site. The material is too heavy and the work too exhausting for one person to do alone. (The only thing the truck driver will do is pour; he won't rake!)

Never pour concrete if you expect temperatures to drop below 40 degrees F. during the next week. That eliminates early spring, late fall, and winter. If temperatures do drop lower, you will have to take precautions to keep the material above that temperature.

Codes and your building plans have the final say, but usually you need concrete of a mix of at least 2000 psi, 28-day strength. If you mix the concrete yourself (and we don't recommend it), you will need a mix of 1:3:5—one part Portland cement, three parts clean sand, and five parts gravel.

To place concrete in footing forms, shovel it in by thin layers. Rake and tamp to remove all air pockets. Continue this process until forms are filled. Tops of footings should be smooth and level all the way around. Use a trowel to adjust surface.

Allow several days for the footings to "cure." Remember, concrete doesn't dry, it sets. Then remove the wood forms, if they were used.

LAYING THE FIRST COURSE OF BLOCKS

Regardless of whether your house is a slab-on-grade, with crawl space or full foundation, the procedure for laying the first course of blocks is the same.

First, find the outside corner of the foundation wall as described earlier. Re-tie strings to locate the corners. Then outline where the blocks will go; use either a piece of chalk or snap a chalk line.

Then lay the bottom course of blocks completely around the perimeter of the footing *without mortar.* This way, you will be able to see where you have to cut blocks to create a good fit. Generally, blocks should be placed an average of one-half inch apart, but this can vary from ⅜ inch to ¾ inch.

With blocks resting in place without mortar, mark the joint locations on the footings with chalk. Then lift the blocks out of the way. Before you actually lay the blocks with mortar, doublecheck to make sure where all plumbing and utility openings will be.

For laying block, a mortar mix is prepared using two parts masonry cement (or one part each of Portland cement and hydrated lime) with four to six parts of damp mortar sand. Water should be added slowly. The consistency should be such that the material clings to the trowel but does not squeeze out when a block is placed on it.

It's suggested that you get at least one helper for this job. Another good bet is to rent a cement mixer. Mixing cement is a backbreaking job without one of these. If you have one helper, he or she can mix the material in the mixer, while you lay block. That way the job will go a lot quicker.

Lay blocks as shown in Illustration 4. To begin, trowel the mortar on the footing and place block on top. Work it into the masonry and check for level. Place the next block as per the chalk mark on the footing. Adjust and level. Now trowel in mortar into the joint between the two blocks and then scrape off any excess. For succeeding courses, you will only place mortar on the face of the block.

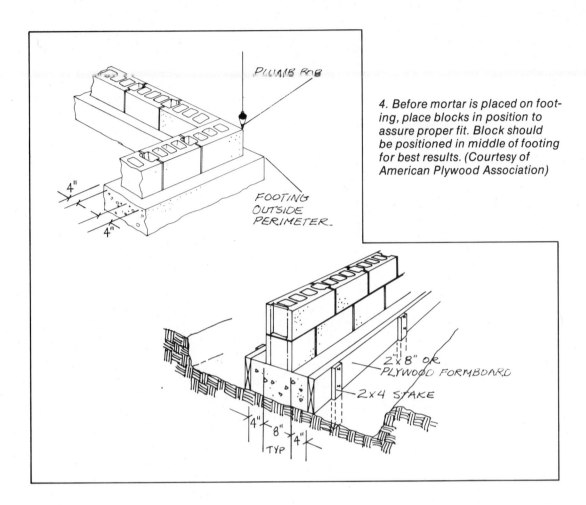

4. Before mortar is placed on footing, place blocks in position to assure proper fit. Block should be positioned in middle of footing for best results. (Courtesy of American Plywood Association)

When adding each new course of blocks, stagger it so that you do not have two joints right above each other. The wall is not built adding on one course upon another; rather, you must build the corners up first to full height to establish required thickness of joints. Use corner blocks with one flat end at corners. Build corners up using a mason's level to keep blocks plumb and level. Then stretch a line between corners to guide the laying of additional blocks.

Before finishing the last two courses of blocks, locate and position anchor bolts as shown on your plans, or as in Illustration 5. You will have to provide at least two bolts per individual sill plate. Fill all cells in the top course with mortar. When the wall is completed, wait at least a week before you backfill against it. Install 2x6 sill plates around perimeter of foundation.

If this seems too much trouble, you might want to investigate a poured concrete foundation wall. It can be used for crawl space, slab-on-grade or for full foundation walls, and is a lot of trouble to do yourself.

You might want to locate a contractor in your area who specializes in this work. He will supply concrete forms, labor and materials. You will save a lot of time and be able to get on with the building of the superstructure more quickly. Depending on your area, a poured concrete foundation is usually competitive with a block foundation. But get bids from two contractors and compare costs yourself.

POSTS AND GIRDERS

In a house, here's the way the supports work. Vertical posts run from the boxed footings and support the horizontal girder. The girder, along with the foundation walls, supports the floor joists which in turn support the interior flooring and loadbearing walls.

Posts are constructed of lumber which are solid pieces of wood either 4x4 or 6x6. Girders are generally constructed of either two or three pieces of dimensional lumber such as 2x8, 2x10 or 2x12.

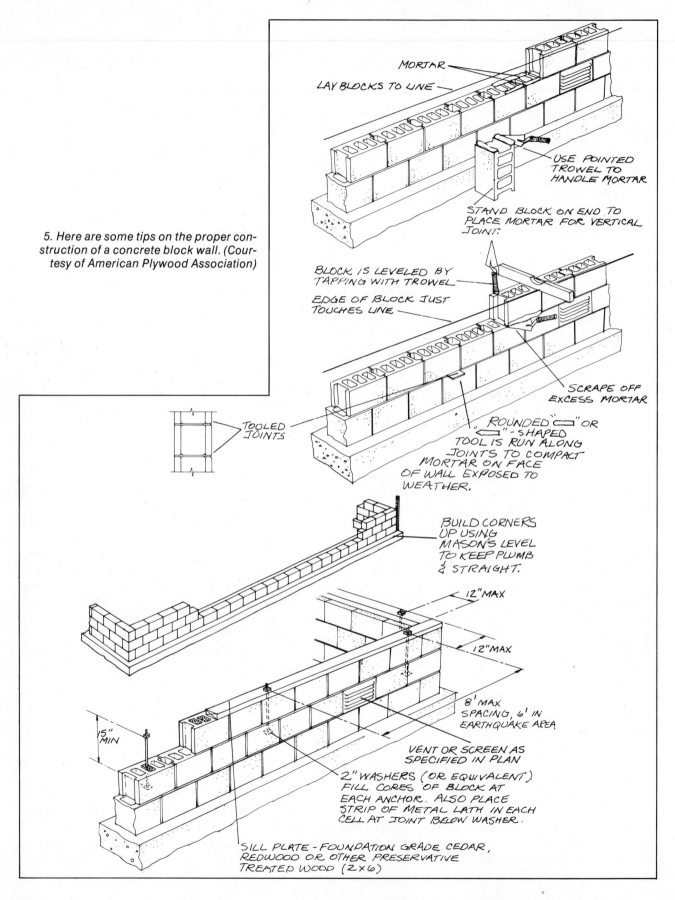

5. Here are some tips on the proper construction of a concrete block wall. (Courtesy of American Plywood Association)

MORTAR

LAY BLOCKS TO LINE

USE POINTED TROWEL TO HANDLE MORTAR

STAND BLOCK ON END TO PLACE MORTAR FOR VERTICAL JOINT.

BLOCK IS LEVELED BY TAPPING WITH TROWEL

EDGE OF BLOCK JUST TOUCHES LINE

SCRAPE OFF EXCESS MORTAR

TOOLED JOINTS

ROUNDED " " OR " "-SHAPED TOOL IS RUN ALONG JOINTS TO COMPACT MORTAR ON FACE OF WALL EXPOSED TO WEATHER.

BUILD CORNERS UP USING MASON'S LEVEL TO KEEP PLUMB & STRAIGHT.

12" MAX

12" MAX

8' MAX SPACING, 6' IN EARTHQUAKE AREA

15" MIN

VENT OR SCREEN AS SPECIFIED IN PLAN

2" WASHERS (OR EQUIVALENT) FILL CORES OF BLOCK AT EACH ANCHOR. ALSO PLACE STRIP OF METAL LATH IN EACH CELL AT JOINT BELOW WASHER.

SILL PLATE—FOUNDATION GRADE CEDAR, REDWOOD OR OTHER PRESERVATIVE TREATED WOOD (2×6)

The long dimension of the house will determine the length of the girder. The girder does not rest on the block foundation but rather just inside it as in Illustration 6. Therefore, if you have a 32-foot long house and you are using 8-inch block, the length of the girder will be 32 feet minus 16 inches (give or take an inch or two for clearance.)

The girder, as a main support of the house, must rest squarely on the posts. In the 32-foot house mentioned above, the center girder would be made in two 16-foot sections using three 2x12 nailed together with 20d (4 foot long) common nails 32 inches o.c. in each of two rows—one along the top and one along the bottom of the girder. Stagger the top and bottom rows as in Illustration 6.

Once the girder is made in sections, you must determine the exact length of the posts. Stretch a line from the sill plate across the designated position for the girder to the other sill plate. Use a strong line which can be stretched tightly. When the string is taut, measure the distance to each footing. Then subtract the dimension of the girder. That's the length of the post. You must make separate measurements for each post because there may be a slight variation. If post footings have a protruding piece of reinforced bar, drill post bottom so that the post can slip over the bar.

Sometimes building codes insist on the installation of a vapor barrier in the crawl space. If this is the case with your house, then install it now and cover the post footings with the material. If not, then place a piece of 15-pound asphalt-impregnated building felt between concrete post footing and the post end. Posts will rest on this material as in Illustration 8.

Once posts are positioned, lift the girder and place it on top of the posts. The girder must be cut so that butt joint falls over the center line of the supporting post, as in Illustration 8. Trim the two end girder sec-

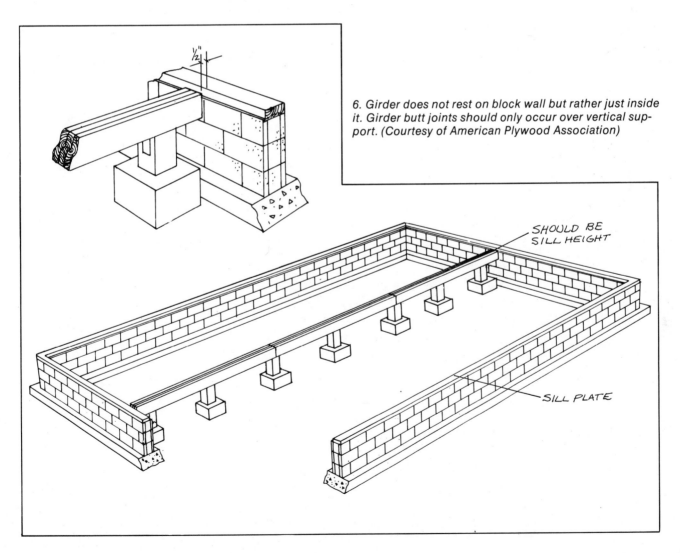

6. Girder does not rest on block wall but rather just inside it. Girder butt joints should only occur over vertical support. (Courtesy of American Plywood Association)

SHOULD BE SILL HEIGHT

SILL PLATE

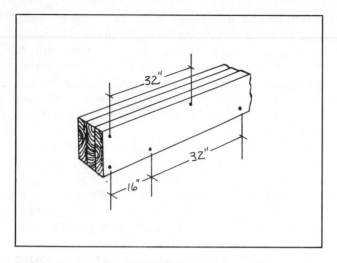

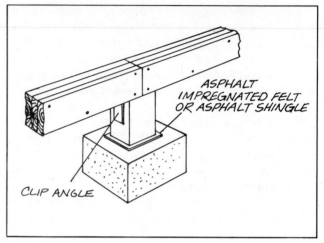

7. Construction detail for making a support girder. (Courtesy of American Plywood Association)

8. If a vapor barrier is not specified by codes, place a piece of 15-pound asphalt-impregnated building felt between concrete post and footing. (Courtesy of American Plywood Association)

9. Begin joist layout at edge of sill plate. Floor joists can only lap over girder. Note construction of opening in floor. (Coutesy of American Plywood Association)

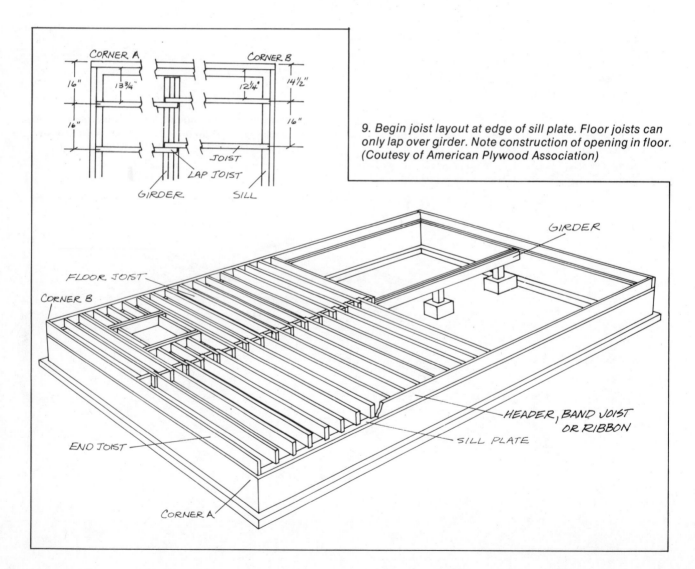

tions to allow for a 1-inch clearance. Unless you are going to immediately install floor joists, brace posts and girder sections with 2x4s to hold them in exact position.

Now check for level. The entire girder must be level with sill plates. If there is a dip or an unlevel spot at one post position, shim between girder and post with a piece of cedar shingle (a few cedar shingles are great to have on the job for such situations). Once level, connect girder and posts. Toenail at least six 10d common nails into post. Then firmly attach the girder to each post on the underside with galvanized steel framing anchors or clip angles which are available from a well-stocked hardware store.

LAYING FLOOR JOISTS

With foundation complete, and sill plates and girder in position, you are ready to begin on the superstructure: that is, everything above the foundation. First, floor joists must be laid. The joists on this level are really the main support of the house. They rest on sill plates, previously installed and center girder.

Typically, floor joists are either 2x8, 2x10 or in special situations 2x12. They are positioned either 16 inches on center or 24 inches on center.

Before this portion of the work begins, check plans and building codes to determine if any special type of wood grade is called for. Sometimes you can use the wrong grade of lumber and not realize it until the building inspector comes around for the framing inspection and informs you.

Often you can save money here by placing the joists 24 inches on center and then use a thicker plywood subfloor. This has to be agreed to by the building inspector.

Another tip to keep in mind: Once you get your order of lumber on site, notice that most joists have a bow and a crown on them; this means that on one edge the lumber is usually slightly warped one way or the other. You must always crown the joists. That means that the side that warps up, must be placed in an up position. Once the floor is in place it will straighten out. If you place the joist with the crown down, you will have a dip in the floor after it is installed. Once you really see what you are looking for, it will only take a moment to crown each joist.

Joist layout depends on plans, but here are several steps to aid you in understanding joist layout.

(1) Begin layout by starting at the edge of sill plate, as in Illustration 9. Use the outside of the sill plate as starting point. Because joists must be located exactly 16 inches on center (unless you are using a 24 inch on center layout), you must calculate the thickness of the joist, then mark on sill plate where the joist would touch. Find the center between the two marks, then measure in 16 inches. This would be the point where the center of the second joist would touch. Continue this all the way along the wall until you reach the end of the house. In each case, you should have about 13 1/2 inches between each joist. Be careful with this. Should you go over the required 16 inches on center, the building inspector is liable to make you put an additional joist between this span.

(2) Once the first side is marked off, you must then mark off the parallel wall in the same manner. All joists must be parallel to one another. (You can begin to see the major problems you would have even now if you did not build the foundation squarely. How do you run floor joists parallel on a foundation which is not square?) Now mark correct joist locations on the center girder.

(3) Go over the floor plans very carefully now. When you come across an interior wall which is running parallel to the floor joists, the wall not only needs to be located on top of a joist but it also needs a double joist positioned to help support this extra weight.

(4) At this time also check plans for openings in the floor. This would include openings for a crawl space or an opening to the basement, if you have a full foundation. You will lay all floor joists the same but you must be aware of where openings will be.

(5) Now install end joists and headers. Select your straightest pieces of lumber for this. End joists and headers form a box around the remainder of the floor joists. The headers, as in Illustration 9, are the beams which fit perpendicularly at the end of the floor joists to form that box. Now nail it off. Use large 16d nails to attach the end joists to the headers. Then, at intervals of 16 inches, toenail the headers and end joists into the sill plates.

(6) Now you are ready to install the other floor joists. Because you have marked off the sill plates, you know the location of each floor joist. To ensure that each joist is square on the vertical, use a steel square and scribe a line on the inside of the header.

(7) Then cut to size and install joists. If lumber does not span entire dimension of the house, then it must overlap over the center girder.

(8) When installing joists, remember that all "crowns" must be facing up. Joists can be secured using two or three 16d nails. Nail through the header and into the floor joist. Toenail joist at girder. If joists overlap at girder, nail them together and also toenail into girder. Overlap should be a minimum of four inches and a maximum of 24 inches.

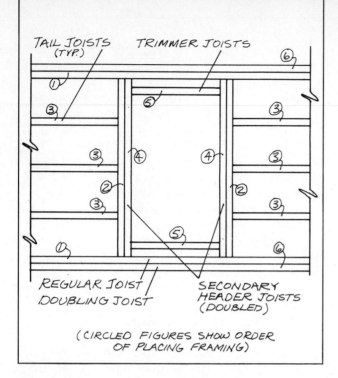

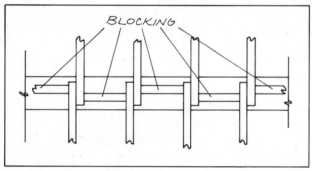

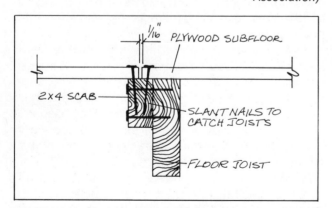

10. Typical framing detail of opening in floor. All joists are positioned and secured, then they are cut and opening is framed out. (Courtesy of American Plywood Association)

11. Once floor joists are in place, they must be blocked. Blocking is merely pieces of lumber secured between joists. Here blocking is placed on centerline girder where joists overlap. (Courtesy of American Plywood Association)

12. If something is out of square and plywood panel does not rest securely on joist, then a piece of 2 x 4 can be nailed to joist. If plywood is substantially short, the panel should be cut to fit closest joist. (Courtesy of American Plywood Association)

(9) Go back and find the floor openings, once all joists are secured. Cut and frame all openings as shown in Illustration 10, or as per house plans. Take care to find the position and cut joists without knocking them out of alignment. Use a double secondary header as shown and end nail into joists.

(10) Floor joists need blocking. Use pieces of lumber the same dimension as floor joists; fit them between joists at girder position. See Illustration 11.

INSTALLING SUBFLOOR

In a typical installation, plywood subfloor is attached to the floor joists. If hardwood flooring is later applied, no additional plywood is needed on floor. If tile or carpet is applied directly to floor, another layer of plywood is needed. This second layer is not added until much later in the construction process.

If you have taken care to build a square foundation and have properly installed floor joists parallel to one another, the job of applying subfloor is easy. Use 4x8 sheets of plywood for this job. Before you cut anything, make a small sketch of the plywood layout so you will know what has to be cut.

Start your layout at the same corner where you began laying the floor joists. The subfloor will run perpendicular to the floor joist layout. Therefore, measure in four feet on the two end joists, then snap a chalk line which cuts across all joists.

Without cutting anything, lay a line of 4x8 plywood panels between the chalk line and the outside header. Leave a space of about 1/16 inch between each panel for expansion. You can calculate this as you go along by fitting a dime between panels. Repeat this until you come to the end of the house. If the last panel overlaps the end joist, you can simply cut it off. If the last panel falls short an inch or two, you will need to install a piece of blocking underneath. Simply hammer a portion of 2x4 on the end joist so that you have something to attach the subfloor to. The end of the plywood always must be supported underneath (see Illustration 12).

Further, in this initial layout of the subfloor, each panel end should rest on the center of the floor joist. If it does not, you have not installed the floor joists properly.

Once this first section of subfloor is in place, you can begin the second course. The subfloor panels must be staggered. That is, when you begin the second course, use half a panel to begin with and then a full panel as in Illustration 13. Leave about ⅛ inch space between courses of subfloor.

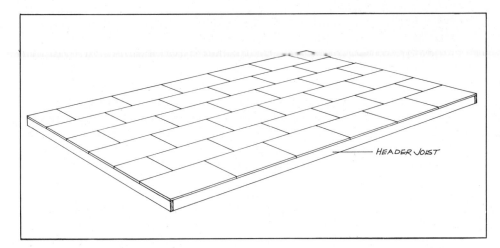

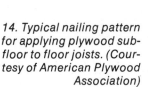

13. Subfloor panels must be staggered. Also, leave about ⅛ inch space between courses of subfloor so that wood has room to expand. (Courtesy of American Plywood Association)

HEADER JOIST

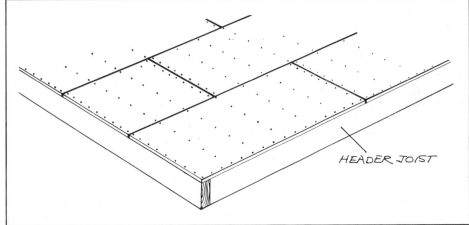

14. Typical nailing pattern for applying plywood subfloor to floor joists. (Courtesy of American Plywood Association)

HEADER JOIST

As you work your way down, remember that all panel ends must rest squarely on floor joists. If something is slightly out of kilter, you can probably correct it by trimming one panel.

Once all panels are in place, you can nail off the subfloor. Probably the easiest way to do this is to go back over your work and accurately snap a chalk line over the location of each floor joist. This will save you time finding the floor joist as you nail, and perhaps keep you from missing the joist altogether.

Use either 6d or 8d nails, nail off the panels. At the ends of panels, drive about 10 nails into it. At intermediate stages drive about five or six nails. Where panels touch headers, space and drive about 17 nails (see Illustration 14). Take care to angle each nail into the joists and headers. If you miss the joists with nails, you could end up with squeaky floors. Once this platform is in place, you can begin work on the sidewalls of the house.

FRAMING THE WALLS

Wall framing includes installation of vertical wall studs, horizontal members called bottom and top plates, window and door headers, and interior walls.

How to build a wall: The most efficient way to build a wall today is construct it on the flat and tip it into place. To do this you really need at least one helper, perhaps more. If there are only two people building walls, do not build one longer than 24 feet or it will be too unwieldy to tip in place. On a small vacation house it is doubtful that you would need a wall any longer than this.

Begin by finding the location of every exterior and interior wall on your plans. Then nail "bottom plates" in those locations. A bottom plate is the bottom horizontal support, made of 2x4, to which the wall studs are nailed. Temporarily nail all bottom plates in proper location. Do not use too many nails because you will have to remove plates later. By determining each wall location, you can figure out where you will need special framing.

With bottom plates in place, begin with exterior walls and find the location of each wall stud. These are placed 16 inches on center. You can determine stud location similarly to floor joists. Measure in 16 inches from the end of the wall. Figure the width of the stud and mark it. Find the center between the two marks. From that center measure another 16 inches. This next mark will be the center of your second stud. Continue to end to find all stud locations (see Illustration 15).

At the end of walls and at intersections you will need to add a second stud. Check your plans for location of this second stud. When calculating stud locations, measure from the outside stud, not from the extra stud (see Illustration 15).

On completing this, cut another series of plates. These will be the bottom section of your "top plates." Top plates are the horizontal members which run along the top of the stud wall. The standard wall is constructed as follows. There is one horizontal bottom plate, vertical wall studs, the two top plates. Once cut, you can place the top plates on top of the bottom plates and keep them together temporarily.

How to cut studs: Generally you can buy precut studs. If possible, use them. They save you time and avoid wasted materials. If you must cut them from larger 2x4s, here's how to do it. Note from your plans the floor to ceiling height of walls. To this add about one inch for underlayment. Then subtract about 4½

inches, which is the thickness of three plates (one bottom and two top plates).

Carefully cut a stud to this length. You can now use this as a pattern for cutting the remaining studs. The next step is to mark on the subfloor the location of every stud wall with chalk. Using the bottom plate as a guide, mark stud locations on top plates. Then remove all plates from a portion of the floor so that you have a place to work. When removing plates, don't mix up the walls. Organize them so that when you finish one wall you can begin on another.

Begin building the long exterior walls first. Lay the bottom plate on edge. Lay the top plate parallel to the bottom plate about a stud's distance away. Then fill in between the plates with as many studs as necessary. All lumber should be on edge. Holding a stud in its exact location, nail through bottom plate, then nail through top plate into stud ends. Use two 16d nails for this. The second section of top plate will be added later.

Now add extra studs where needed. If the wall section you are building has a window in it, you should now install header and supports as specified on plans. Then make sure the wall section is square by measuring diagonals. Remember, if the wall is in square, the diagonals will be equal.

PLYWOOD WALLS AND SIDING

You have several options now. If you are going to use a siding other than plywood panels, you can now add sheathing, then tip walls into place (your siding

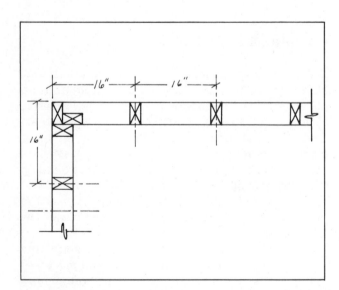

15. Pattern for wall stud layout. (Courtesy of American Plywood Association)

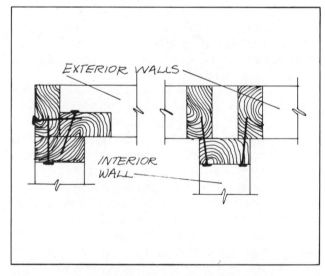

16. At walls and intersections a second stud must be added. Here are typical layouts. (Courtesy of American Plywood Association)

will be added later.) It's recommended, however, that you use plywood panel siding. First, you can save the cost of sheathing walls, because a single plywood siding panel will do the trick. You can also save the labor of siding later (see Illustration 17).

Using plywood panels in this way is called "single-wall" construction. Usually you need a substantial panel for this operation, such as ⅝ inch thick. But your plans and/or building code has the final say here.

The American Plywood Association offers the following suggestions for installing plywood siding panels in the single-wall framing method.

First, siding panels must be cut to proper length. Be careful in determining length so that you do not waste material. You must allow at least one inch lap

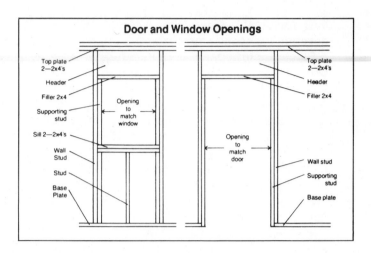

Door and Window Openings

17. Walls can be easily made on the flat, then tipped into place. (Courtesy of American Plywood Association)

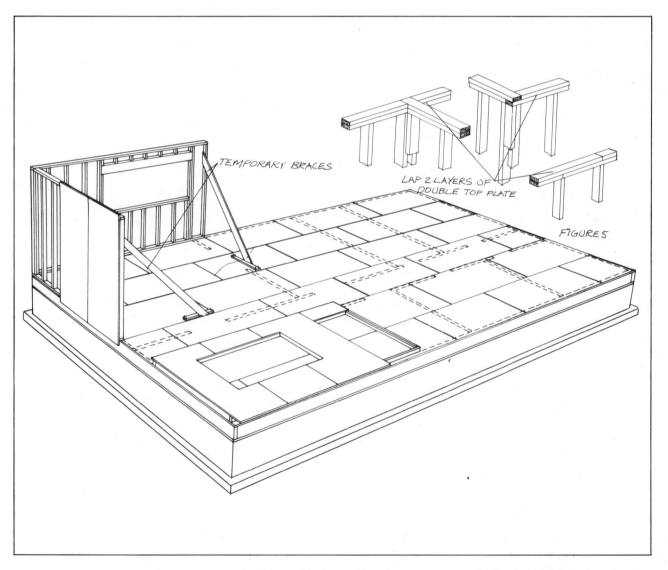

18. After wall is tipped into place, temporarily hold it in place with 2 x 4 lumber. (Courtesy of American Plywood Association)

over the top of the foundation wall and 1½ inches for covering the second top plate.

Place the first panel at one end of the stud wall while it is still on the flat. Make sure edge of panel is flush with the outside edge of the corner stud.

Apply the panel to the wall framing. Use hot-dip galvanized, aluminum, or other nonstaining nails to prevent stain from forming on the siding.

Use 6d box, siding or casing nails for plywood siding that is ½ inch or less in thickness; use 8d nails for thicker panels. Drive nails every 12 inches at intermediate supports. All edges of panel siding must be backed by solid lumber framing and blocking.

Between panels, leave a 1/16 inch gap for expansion. If you force panels in close together, they will eventually buckle. Once wall is sided, tip it into place. You need help to do this right; you could lose control of a heavy wall when you are tilting it into place. With wall tilted and steadied, nail through the bottom plate into the subfloor and header or end joist. Temporarily hold this wall in place by using 2x4 bracing which can be nailed to one of the wall studs and toenailed into the subfloor with the aid of a small block (see Illustration 18).

Other long sidewalls can be constructed in a similar manner. When it comes to adding the walls which make right angles with the longer walls mentioned above, a different procedure is necessary. The plywood panels of those walls do not butt the end as above. Rather the panel must extend past the end of the wall in order to cover the end of the larger wall as shown in Illustration 19.

The best way to handle this is to build the smaller wall and tip it into place and fasten it. Then apply the panel. Usually you can purchase and install corner trim pieces in case the fit is not exact.

When walls are in place, joints can be caulked. You don't have to caulk shiplapped joints. But you do have to caulk butt joints at inside and outside wall corners. Use a good grade caulk for this so that you do not have to recaulk it in another year.

Once all exterior walls are in place, you can build the interior walls the same way. They are not covered with anything at this point. Bare stud walls should be built and installed.

Once you are sure every wall is plumb and square, you can add the second set of top plates. Then you can move on to framing the ceiling.

FRAMING THE CEILING

In a simple house, such as the one described here, ceiling joists are installed similarly to floor joists. They span from one exterior wall, over loadbearing interior walls, to the other side of the house. There are many different design motifs, including sloped roofs, cathedral ceilings, etc. Here, we'll discuss a flat ceiling.

The ceilings joists have several functions: tie the walls in together, offer a structure upon which to apply ceiling material, and support a second-story floor in a two-story house.

19. Construction detail shows attachment of sidewall to longer wall. (Courtesy of American Plywood Association)

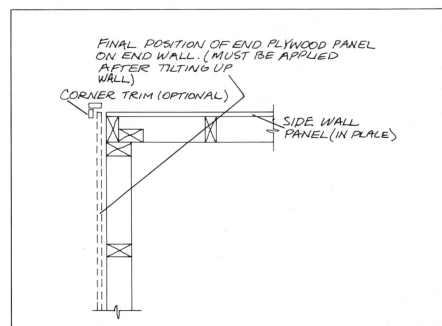

FINAL POSITION OF END PLYWOOD PANEL ON END WALL. (MUST BE APPLIED AFTER TILTING UP WALL)

CORNER TRIM (OPTIONAL)

SIDE WALL PANEL (IN PLACE)

Although we are only describing a single-story vacation house here, if you add a plywood subfloor on top of the ceiling joists you will have extra storage space. At some point you might also want to add dormers and create an extra sleeping space.

The only difference in construction between laying floor joists and laying ceiling joists is that you do not use headers with the ceiling joists. Joists are positioned as per your plans and building codes. Typically, floor joists are positioned 16 inches on center. Many codes allow ceiling joists to be positioned 24 inches on center.

Except for short spans, ceiling joists need support. This support is usually provided by loadbearing interior walls (all interior walls which run perpendicular to floor joists are loadbearing). Where there are broad expanses of space, a beam must be provided for ceiling joist support. Your plans will detail this. If a beam is indicated and it is located below ceiling joists, the joists rest on it. If it is on the same level or above, the joists are hung from the beam with the help of metal hangers. This would be specified on plans.

In a small house, you can usually secure lumber which will span the entire distance. If not, then joists must lap over an interior loadbearing wall—no place else. If they do overlap, then you must consider roof rafter position immediately. Roof rafters must always frame opposite each other, but this would be impossible to do with a simple joist overlap.

There is a good solution to this. Layout the ceiling joists and place a block, the same dimensions as roof rafters, between the joist overlap (see Illustration 20). Then the roof rafters can be installed on either side of the ceiling joists and thus frame opposite each other over the filler block.

Because the end roof rafter must sit flush with the outside wall, it will not lap with the end ceiling joist. Therefore, it is usually easier to fit the end joists in after the gable end has been framed out. So start your ceiling joist layout approximately 24 inches in from the end, if you are locating ceiling joists 24 inches on center (see Illustration 21). Then continue placing them at specified distances until you get to the other end. You can calculate ceiling joist positions in a similar manner to the way you calculated floor joist positions.

When measuring and cutting the ceiling joists, measure from the outside of the exterior wall to the center interior loadbearing wall or beam. Leave an extra four to six inches for an overlap with filler block and the other joist. Place joists with crown up. Then toenail joists into exterior top plate and interior wall top plate. Use 10d nails for this. Then with 16d nails, nail through the joist and into the filler block. Do the

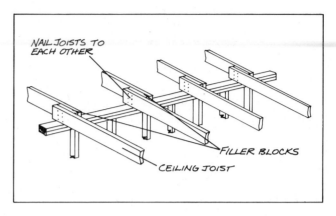

20. Lap ceiling joists over support. (Courtesy of American Plywood Association)

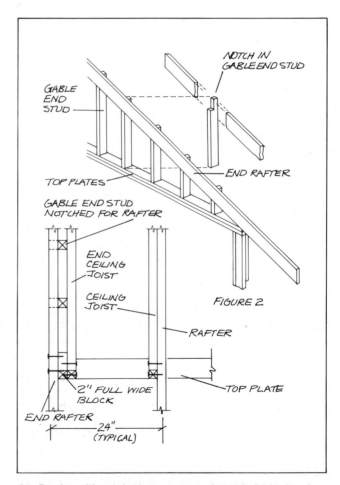

21. Begin ceiling joist layout approximately 24 inches in from roof end. End joist is added later. (Courtesy of American Plywood Association)

same with the other joist meeting the filler block so that you have a strong connection. If the joists touch any other interior wall, toenail into that as well.

Now, access to the attic must be cut and framed out similarly to openings through the main floor into the crawl space or basement. Eventually the ends of the ceiling joists will have to be trimmed to fit the slope of the roof rafters, but you can do that after the rafters are installed.

Sheets of plywood should be temporarily (but firmly) fastened to the top side of the ceiling joists so that you have solid footing for installation of the roof rafters.

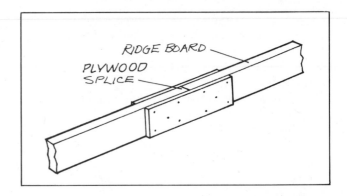

22. Typical attachment for ridge board. To join two portions of ridge board, make a plywood gusset and nail as shown. (Courtesy of American Plywood Association)

INSTALLING ROOF RAFTERS

Up to now the building of this small house has been rather straightforward and relatively simple. Cutting and installing roof rafters is probably the most complicated part of building a house. You should not undertake this part of construction without the help of at least one other person. In fact, that one other person should be a carpenter who has had experience with this.

Framing out the roof not only involves construction and placement of roof rafters, but also construction and placement of cripple studs, ridge board and collar beams.

As described in the previous section, roof rafter locations should be determined at the same time that ceiling joist locations are set. If you have done this, then the exact position of roof rafters (to fit over the filler block) will be apparent.

Cutting and placing of roof rafters is made somewhat complicated because you have to take the slope of the roof into account. Your home plans will detail this slope for you. Usually the rise is between four to six inches per foot. That is, the roof pitch will increase four inches for each foot as you move toward the center of the house. On a house which is 24 feet wide, the peak would occur at 12 feet. Multiplying four inches by 12 feet, you can calculate that the roof rises 48 inches.

The real complication comes because the roof rafters must be cut at an angle that properly meets the ridge board (main beam running the length of the house). You must also notch-cut the rafters so that they fit into and are seated with the exterior wall top plate. Finally, you must have the proper overhang, as specified on your plans.

The best way to begin is to draw a full-scale sideview of the rafter construction right onto your plywood subfloor. Set it up so that you take the ridge

beam, top plates and slope into account. Once this is done, take two of the pieces of lumber you will use for roof rafters and lay them on top of the drawing. Now draw in the cuts you will have to make. Check carefully, then make the cuts as needed. Set them up on the subfloor in the same manner you would on the roof to see if they fit together properly. Once you have a good fit (don't forget the width of the ridge beam in this test), you can use these two rafters as patterns upon which to cut the remaining pieces.

If you have a perfectly square house, you can now cut all the remaining rafters. If you do not have confidence that everything is exact, you may want to cut just a few at first to help support the ridge beam. Then you can fit the pattern rafters in place; if they fit exactly, you can then cut more rafters. If they do not, then you will have to adjust your cut as you go along the length of the house.

The ridge board must be fabricated. In a very small house, the ridge board can be one piece of lumber. In most cases, you will have to use several pieces. Check your plans to determine what size beam you need for the ridge board (see Illustration 22).

Select your straightest pieces of lumber for the ridge board. Construct it in several sections, whether on the ground or on the subfloor platform. Take the sections, some 2x4 supports, and several sets of roof rafters, up to the top of the house. With one or more helpers, nail the temporary support in place at the end of the house on the top plate. Place another support in about the distance of the first length of ridge board, and nail it to a ceiling joist.

With the temporary supports nailed at the bottom, check the ridge board section for level. Then firmly hold the ridge board while assistants toenail it to the temporary supports. Also at this time install enough diagonal bracing to ensure that the ridge board will

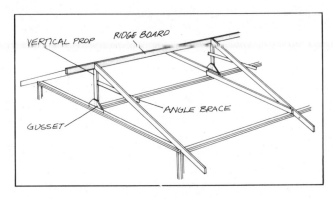

23. With helpers and supports place ridge board. Then add several pairs of rafters to help hold in place. (Courtesy of American Plywood Association)

not move. Now double check for level. (Illustration 23).

Install the first set of rafters at the end of the house by toenailing them into the ridge board and into the top plate. Install the next set of rafters in a similar fashion, near the end of the ridge board section. Then install the next ridge board section and rafters. Continue to the end of the house.

The ridge board sections must be joined securely. Make plywood gussets (one for each side of the joint). They should be the width of the board and have enough overlap to enable you to nail it securely.

Again, check the ridge board for level and to be sure the board is centered over the house. Now install the remaining rafters in pairs. As you install the rafters, continue to check for level and straightness. This cannot be stressed enough. A crooked ridge board can ruin the whole look of the house. When installing rafters, never force one against the ridge board; this could throw it off of center.

Rafters should be nailed to the top plate; you can use 10d nails for this. Then using 16d nails, nail rafters to ridge board. Also nail rafters into floor joists. In high wind areas you may want to add extra metal stripping. But consult your architect or building inspector on this point.

As in Illustration 24, cut and nail 1x6 collar beams in place for every other roof rafter in the upper third of the rafter.

If vents are to be installed at the ends of the roof, find the center line from the ridge board to top plate. Measure the vent to be installed and leave half this distance on either side of your mark. Install your first set of studs taking into account the width of the vent. Then continue to install studs 16 inches on center. The top end of the stud should be cut to fit under the rafter. The stud bottom should fit flush with the top plate. Cut and frame out vent opening (Illustration 25).

Install outside ceiling joists on the inside of the end stud wall. Install fascia board, which will correct the length of the ridge board. Check your plans on this, then install fascia rafters to cover the end of the ridge board.

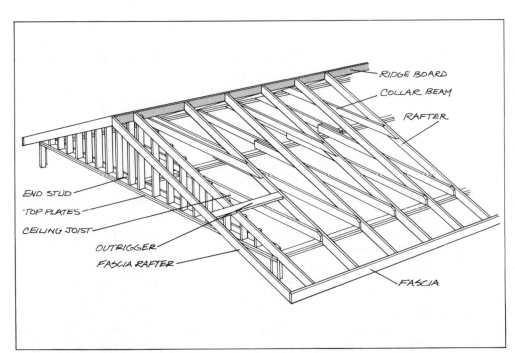

24. Cut and nail collar beams in place. (Courtesy of American Plywood Association)

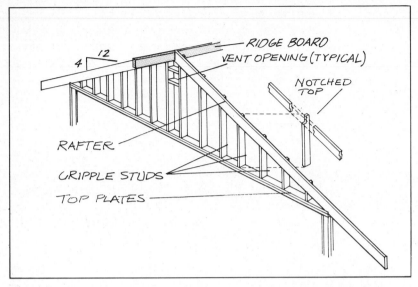

25. Frame out roof end and create vent opening if necessary. (Art Courtesy of American Plywood Association)

26. Make layout of sheathing positioning to cut down on waste. (Art Courtesy of American Plywood Association)

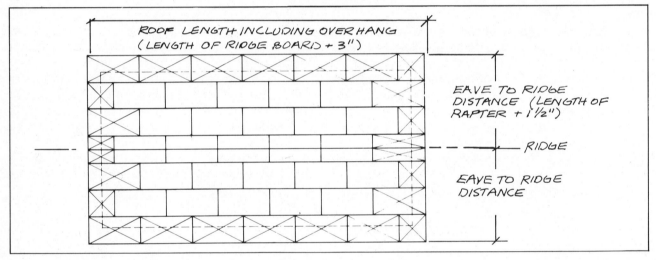

INSTALLING ROOF SHEATHING

Installing roof sheathing is no more difficult than installing sublfooring, except that you are working up in the air. You can install full panels of plywood that must be staggered in the same fashion as the floor sheathing. It is best to do a sketch of the layout first. That way you can avoid waste (see Illustration 26).

Start panel installation at any corner of the roof. It is usually suggested that you use 6d common smooth nails. They can be spaced six inches on center along the ends of panels and 12 inches on center at intermediate supports. As with subflooring, leave about 1/16 inch space at panel ends and ⅛ inch at edge joints for possible expansion.

Your plans will show either open soffits or closed soffits. In you have open soffits, you will have to be careful to use short-enough nails on the roofing ma-

terial so that you do not puncture the plywood and leave unsightly nail ends showing (see Illustration 27).

ROOF COVERING

On the pitched roof described in the last section, one of the most economical roof coverings is asphalt shingles. Today, these shingles come in a great variety of colors and textures so that you are relatively sure of finding one to fit in to your design scheme. Of course, you can always use cedar shingles. Although quite beautiful, they are also very expensive. This section will discuss the application of asphalt shingles.

To begin, you need to erect a type of scaffolding so that you can bring shingles to the roof area and also have room to work. A local hardware store or equipment rental firm will be able to help you with this.

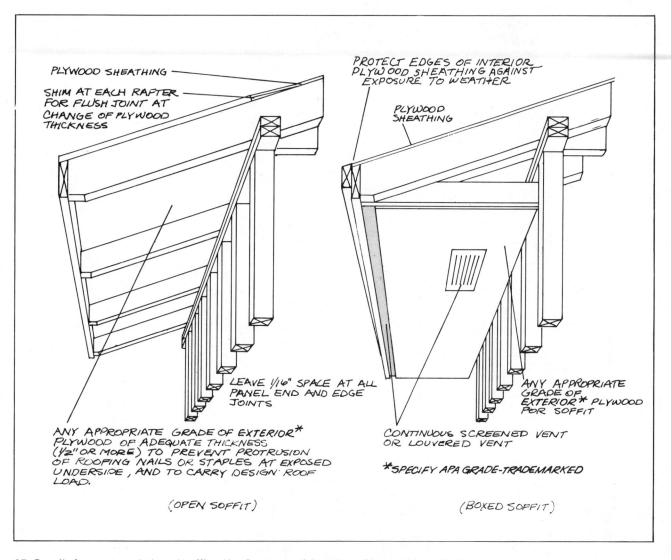

PLYWOOD SHEATHING

SHIM AT EACH RAFTER FOR FLUSH JOINT AT CHANGE OF PLYWOOD THICKNESS

LEAVE 1/16" SPACE AT ALL PANEL END AND EDGE JOINTS

ANY APPROPRIATE GRADE OF EXTERIOR* PLYWOOD OF ADEQUATE THICKNESS (1/2" OR MORE) TO PREVENT PROTRUSION OF ROOFING NAILS OR STAPLES AT EXPOSED UNDERSIDE, AND TO CARRY DESIGN ROOF LOAD.

(OPEN SOFFIT)

PROTECT EDGES OF INTERIOR PLYWOOD SHEATHING AGAINST EXPOSURE TO WEATHER

PLYWOOD SHEATHING

ANY APPROPRIATE GRADE OF EXTERIOR* PLYWOOD FOR SOFFIT

CONTINUOUS SCREENED VENT OR LOUVERED VENT

*SPECIFY APA GRADE-TRADEMARKED

(BOXED SOFFIT)

27. Details for open and closed soffits. (Art Courtesy of American Plywood Association)

Next, the roof must be swept clean of all debris. Check for any irregularities and correct. Never begin roofing unless the area is absoultely dry.

An underlayment of roofing felt is applied to the sheathing. This can be stapled into place. Typically, the felt comes in rolls about three feet wide. Roll one course out and secure. Then roll the next course out and lap it over the previous course, with an overlap of at least four inches of material.

Areas such as the peak of the roof, which are likely to take water, should be flashed. This is a strip of non-corrosive metal which overlaps the peak and helps prevent water from leaking into the house. On more elaborate houses, where there are a number of peaks and valleys, extensive flashing is needed.

Before you actually start to shingle, distribute bundles along the roof. Shingles come in bundles, and three bundles equal a square which covers 100 square feet of roof area. Usually shingles are 12 inches by 36 inches. Five of the twelve are exposed to the weather, while a full seven inches overlaps as in Illustration 28.

Shingling begins at the low point of the roof—at the eaves, working up toward the ridge. A row of shingles is applied, the next row overlaps, and so on up. Carefully measure up 12 inches from the eave and snap a chalk line along the roof. This acts as a guide for applying shingles in a straight line.

Nail the starter course. Use hot-dipped galvanized nails, two for each tab or six nails for each shingle. Once the starter course is in place, again snap a chalk line and apply the second course. Remember that you must have seven inches of overlap, so take that into account when positioning the chalk line. Although you can shingle a roof yourself, having a helper makes it a lot easier—even something as simple as snapping a chalk line goes twice as fast.

This is a quick, basic course in roofing. For special and more difficult situations, it is safest to consult a professional.*

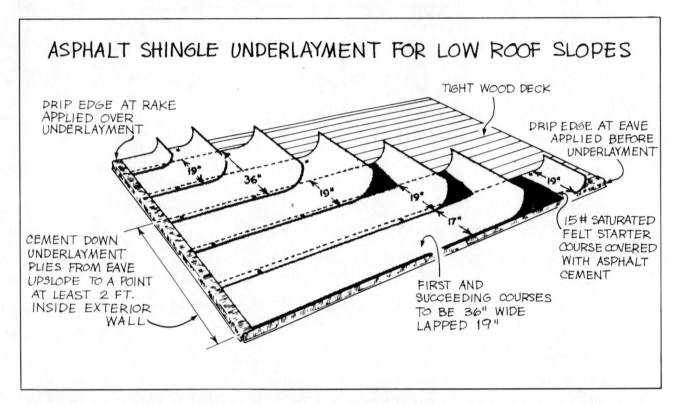

28. Low-Slope Application of asphalt shingles ranging from 2-in-12 up to (but not including) 4-in-12 should have a cemented-down felt underlayment as indicated in this drawing. According to the Asphalt Roofing Manufacturers Association, the cementing-down should extend up the slope to a point at least two feet inward from the inside face of the exterior wall. Asphalt roofing cement is applied at the approximate rate of two gallons per hundred square feet between deck and felt, and between felt layer and felt layer. Use a comb-type trowel to spread the cement.

A WEATHERTIGHT HOUSE

Once the roof shingles are in place, windows and doors should be added to make the house weathertight and secure. The best bet for the do-it-yourselfer is to purchase prehung windows and doors. These units come already in frames. Typically, they are fitted into the rough opening (created during framing). Blocks of wood are placed around the unit which is then leveled and secured. Relatively inexpensive interior doors also come this way and can be quickly installed.

Sliding glass doors usually come in a package and must be assembled. Units can be assembled on the flat and then tipped into place. Usually they are bolted to the structure.

*Also see Successful Roofing & Siding by Robert C. Reschke.

29. Asphalt Shingle terminology includes the roofing terms indicated. Whether a homeowner contracts the work or does it himself, he should acquaint himself with the basic fundamentals of the work so that he can talk intelligently with contractors or suppliers. The drawings here come from the "Asphalt Shingle Installation Manual" put out by the Asphalt Roofing Manufacturers Assn.

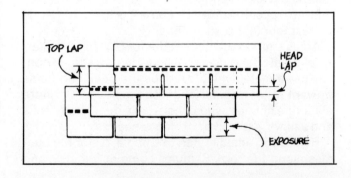

DORMERS AND SKYLIGHTS
FOR SUNLIT ROOMS

Attic space always is small for an obvious reason: the roof slopes. If you are willing to raise one sloping side of the roof you can create a shed-type dormer and a room that runs the entire length of the house.

Then you can put some real magic into it by adding a skylight, or two, or three.

If you want to do this, first check the floor of the attic. Throughout the house, builders have put studs and joists 16 inches on center. But the attic floor often has joists 24 inches on center because the assumption is that few people will be walking around up there. You'll have to fill in the floor of the attic with extra joists; toe-nail them in so they are solid and will support whatever weight you will put into your new room.

The dormer may have a roof high enough to have a separate ceiling, but in many cases you will simply finish off the underside of the roof, insulate it and sheath it so it can serve as the ceiling.

If you want the special magic of skylights, you can install them yourself in the new dormer roof—or any other part of the roof. A fact few people realize is that you can install a skylight even in an unfinished attic, for the room below the attic. The way to do this is to install the skylight in the roof, then construct a simple plywood "light shaft" through the attic crawl space to the room below (see Illustration 30).

There are several brands and types of skylights, including some that can be opened for ventilation. The instructions here showing installation procedure apply to other types, but these are by *Sky-master*, for the plastic "bubble" type. Note one version is "curb-mounted," which raises it slightly above roof level, and the other fits cleanly into the roofing shingles.

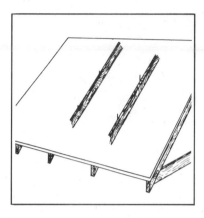

30. Allow yourself 2 to 4 hours of clear weather for the job. To install Skymaster low-profile skylight, which fits cleanly in with shingles and has no curb, drive 3-in. nail up through the roof at the four corners marking the location of your skylight. Be sure there are no electrical wires, pipes or ducts in the way.

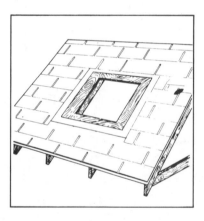

Go up on the roof, locate the nails protruding through, and remove roofing material back about 12 in. around the area. Cut hole through the roof decking.

Plastic skylights of this type are usually fixed in their permanent mountings and do not open to ventilate. Some manufacturers offer units having a flat diffuser sheet with dead air space between it and the domed portion for better insulative properties.

Frame the opening, top and bottom. Rafters will form the sides of the framing. If you are using a bigger skylight and rafters run through the opening, cut the rafter back to make room for the new framing.

Apply roofing mastic around the opening about ¼ in. thick, covering all exposed wood and felt. Use a black roofing mastic such as GAF, Johns-Manville, Bird & Son, or similar.

Apply mastic over the felt strips and replace shingles. After shingles are in place, apply mastic across the bottom of the skylight, as shown in small drawing at lower left.

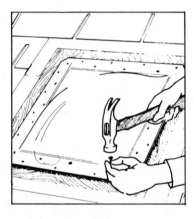

Position skylight over the opening. Drill small holes for the nails. Nail each corner down in line with the rafter, with a 6d or 8d nail. Use ¾-in. rustproof roofing nails around the flange, about 3 in. apart.

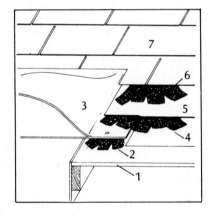

This drawing shows the sequence of materials; 1, roof deck; 2, mastic; 3, skylight; 4, mastic; 5, roofing felt; 6, mastic; 7, shingles.

Apply mastic over the edge of skylight right up to the bubble. Cut strips of roofing felt wide enough to go from the bubble to overlap the felt on the deck. Apply more mastic over these strips at the top and apply the top strip of felt. Don't put a strip on the bottom.

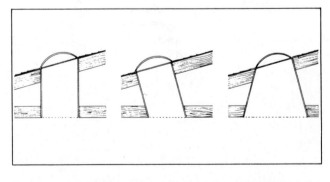

If you want to make a light shaft you can angle it to direct the sunlight. Straight down is best, but if there is some obstruction you can avoid it by angling the shaft. You also might want to make the bottom of the shaft bigger to distribute the light over a broader area. You can use ¼-in. plywood or hardboard for the shaft, paint the inside white, leave the bottom open or·cut a plastic diffuser to cover it.

ALTERNATIVE: The curb model

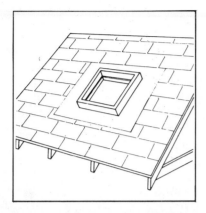

For a curb-type skylight, steps 1 through 4 are the same as for low-profile model. (See preceding pages). Then construct the curb with 2x6 lumber. This will go on top of the roof deck, so inside dimensions of curb will be same as the opening. Be sure to use mastic in all joints.

Replace shingles.

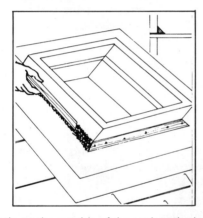

Apply mastic on the outside of the curb at the bottom, and nail cant strips in place. These are triangular moldings that will hold the curb in place.

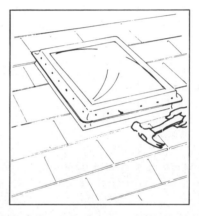

Apply a bead of clear mastic around the top edge of the curb and press skylight down into place. Drill small holes for nails or screws and secure flange around edge about every 3 in.

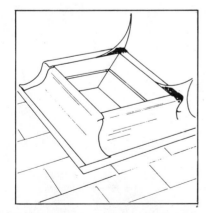

Cover entire outside of curb with mastic, then cover with strips of roofing felt. First put on the bottom one, then the sides, then the top. Be sure to apply mastic everywhere the felt overlaps, and cover all exposed seams with mastic.

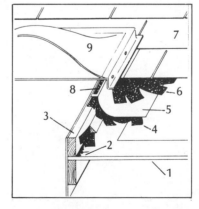

Sequence here is: 1, roof deck; 2, mastic; 3, curb; 4, mastic; 5, roofing felt; 6, mastic; 7, shingles; 8, clear mastic; 9, skylight.

MECHANICAL AND ELECTRICAL

When the house is weathertight, rough mechanical and rough electrical can be installed. In virtually every area of the country, skilled and licensed contractors are required. These jobs must be completed before the walls can be closed up.

WALL COVERING

The two basic types of wall covering or wall finish are plaster and gypsum board. Generally, the wallboard is easier to install yourself. Because it comes in 4x8, 4x10 and 4x12 sheets, you definitely need a helper or two.

In fact, if you have never applied wallboard before, you might want to subcontract it out. Although the actual installation is not difficult, tapping and spackling the joints is difficult for a beginner to finish properly. And if there is anything which gives a new house a sloppy look, it is walls that are poorly finished (see Illustration 31).

If you decide to do it yourself, here's how it is done. Wallboard is installed so that the 8 foot side of the 4x8 sheet is laid on the horizontal. Begin the first panel at a corner of the room. Nail through the wallboard directly into the stud about four to six inches on center. Give the nail an extra hit so that the head of it is below the surface of the board.

The panels can only butt over a stud, never in between. Once the first panel is in place, the second can be added along side it. Panels must always be staggered, which means that you will have to cut a panel in half for the second level. Cut the 4x8 panel so that you have two sections of 4x4. Tip it into place and nail.

Watch out for electrical and mechanical fixtures in the wall. You will have to make a cut in the wallboard as you go along for these fixtures.

Basically, wallboard is applied to ceilings in the same way. Wallboard must run perpendicular to ceiling joists. Each new course must be staggered and panels must only butt over a joist.

When wallboard is in place, metal angles are nailed into all corners. Then tape and spackle can be applied.

Spackle cannot be applied in cold weather. Where two panels butt, spackle is applied in a long strip. Then tape is worked into it with the help of a spackling knife. Spackle is then applied over the tape and pressed firmly over the joint. Excess spackle is then removed. Spackle is again applied after the first coating dries. Repeat this procedure two or three times, until the joint is as smooth as the rest of the wall.

The same procedure applies to corners where two panels meet. Where nails have been driven, spackle is applied over them to smooth out the wall.

FLOORING

There are a variety of flooring types you can add to your house. Oak wood flooring requires a skilled craftsman and special tools.

If you are going to finish your own floor, try a tile or carpeting. Unlike oak floor, tile and carpeting require

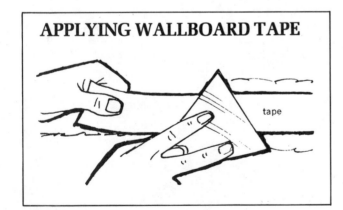

APPLYING WALLBOARD TAPE

31A. Take your wallboard tape, center it over the joint and press the tape firmly, into the bedding compound with your wallboard knife held at a 45° angle. The pressure should squeeze some compound from under the tape, but enough must be left for a good bond.

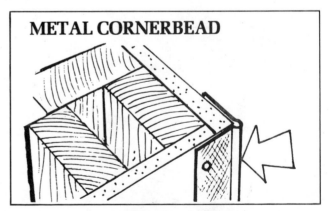

METAL CORNERBEAD

31B. To protect corners from edge damage, install metal cornerbead after you have installed the wallboard. Nail the metal cornerbead every 5" through gypsum board into wood framing.

Gypsum wallboard can be cut with a utility knife, using a 4-foot T-square to assure an accurate cut.

In horizontal wall application of gypsum wallboard, the top panel should be installed first, pushing it flush to the ceiling.

Paper tape and joint compound are applied with a wide knife.

Photos: Georgia-Pacific Corporation

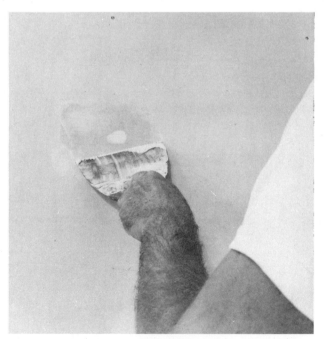

A 4-inch joint finishing knife is used to hide nails below the wallboard surface.

another layer of plywood to make the floor firm. Then these finishes can be applied.

FINISHING THE HOUSE

There are a great many other things you will wish to do to your new vacation house. Some you can do yourself, others you will need help with. Installing appliances and fixtures is better left to a professional while painting or staining your new siding can be completed yourself.

Before you undertake such a project it is suggested that you do more reading on the subject and fully understand your house plans before you begin.*

Once again, if you are going to build a vacation house yourself, keep the over-all project small and keep the design simple. Remember, it takes a carpenter years to develop his skills. And one final word of advice: have someone in the area who is knowledgeable in construction to help you if you get stuck. This can be a local architect, builder, or remodeler. These people would be more than glad to meet with you at the building site and give you advice...for a fee of course.

* *See* How to Build Your Own Home by Robert C. Reschke.

6
Building a
Log Cabin

Log cabins have been a sturdy tradition since the colonists first set foot in America. Recent years have seen a revival in this mode of building. For some people it's probably a genuine pioneering spirit but for most others the idea is grounded in economics: a log cabin is relatively inexpensive and it's a form of building which even a beginner with little or no construction experience can undertake. If you look at the list of manufacturers at the end of this book, you will see that log cabin kit-packaging has become a rather large business, with suppliers in virtually every part of the country. Another indication that this form of building is catching on is the long waiting list, which increases the time between order of the kit and its delivery.

It is possible to build a log cabin from scratch. All you need is a good vacation-home site with plenty of mature trees. Then you can fell as many trees as you need, strip the bark, and let them season. Then use a tractor—or better yet, a good team of horses or oxen—to drag the trees out of the forest and onto the building site. Then you can notch log ends, hoist them into place and before you know it—you have a log cabin...Yes, log cabins can be built from scratch, but we don't recommend it unless you have plenty of time, physical strength, and the willingness and ability to labor long and hard. This chapter will be limited, therefore, to the construction of a log cabin from a kit.*

ARE YOU READY FOR A LOG CABIN?

Although log cabins can be built by a person with little knowledge of construction, it should not be undertaken by a rank amateur. If you want a log cabin, but don't know your way around a construction

*For details on all aspects of log home construction, see Successful Log Homes by James Ritchie.

site, it might be advisable to purchase materials from one of the factories which can also supply you with a construction foreman at a cost. This individual will come to your building site and direct the construction effort. The only talents you and your helpers must have are strong backs and a willingness to follow directions.

Before the kit arrives, a foundation needs to be constructed (see Chapter 5). This can be a full foundation, slab-on-grade, piers or crawl space. Although you can select the type of foundation you want, see what suggestions the kit factory has. Also, the foundation must be constructed to exactly fit the log kit. Therefore, be sure you know both the inside and outside dimensions. Have a thorough discussion with the factory representative, and make sure you understand exactly what is called for.

Before the kit arrives, you will also need a solid road in place so that the big flatbed trailer carrying your future house can get up to the foundation site. If the truck cannot negotiate your road, the kit will be dropped off at the closest possible point. That means you or helpers will have to drag thousands of pounds of logs to the site...a back-breaking and costly job.

People who have constructed log home kits seem to feel that their chief benefits are their easy assembly and their slightly lower cost compared to conventional construction.

SELECTING A SUPPLIER

Your choice of a log home kit will be limited in part by the number of factories which deliver in your area. Once you have determined who will deliver, you can figure out what you want. Most factories sell a variety of different log kits. There are many low-cost kits available which are truly log cabins. That is, units with only one or two rooms. Factories also sell far larger units with two stories and three or four bedrooms. If you want a low-cost vacation home, stick to the

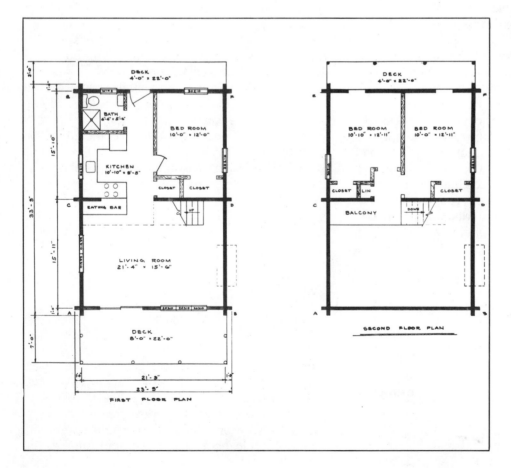

Log cabins fit in well with vacation or leisure-home life styles. This home is a chalet with one bath and three bedrooms. (Art Courtesy of Real Log Homes.)

smaller units. They will be a lot less costly and far easier to build.

Take the time to visit the factory or a local dealer and walk through the model log homes. That's really the only way you can tell if it is large enough or too large for you. Ask the factory representative if these models are designed so that you can start out with a small unit and add to it in a few years. There are such models available.

Although suppliers have different payment schedules, most will want some money at the time the kit is ordered, and the remainder on delivery. If you are going to need a mortgage to finance this project, make sure the bank understands that you need a lot of money before construction. Banks hate to lend money before the house is built. Most like to give you payments at each stage; after the foundation is complete, after framing is finished, and so on. Factories, however, are in business to make money and most have strict payment rules. For example, in many cases the driver has orders not to release the binders and chains holding the logs until he receives two certified checks: one for balance due and the other for delivery charges. Financial details need to be worked out long before the logs arrive.

A road for access to your site is essential. Be sure to have plenty of help at the construction site when your new log home arrives. (Photo Courtesy of Vermont Log Buildings, Inc.)

RECEIVING A DELIVERY

We'll assume that all the financial problems have been worked out, foundation and platform have been installed and you are waiting to take delivery of your new log home. Have three, four or more people there with you. Invite some of your city friends up to your vacation home site, or hire some local people. Whatever you do, don't go it alone.

There have been cases where a poor, unsuspecting log cabin builder waited for delivery himself. When this has happened the driver (who usually won't carry logs) ends up dumping the logs on the ground. Not only do some logs get chipped and split, but they all wind up getting soiled. It creates an avoidable mess.

When the truck arrives, all breakable items should be stored out of the way of the truck in a secure and relatively dry place. Then the logs and all other items can be placed on the ground once a carpet of hay has been spread. Logs and other structural members should be separated and stored according to length and function.

Once you take delivery of the log kit, you have the same problem that others regularly involved in construction have: there are thousands of dollars of building materials laying out on an unprotected site.

Log homes come in many different styles, and are popular in both rural and suburban areas. (Photos courtesy of Vermont Log Buildings, Inc.)

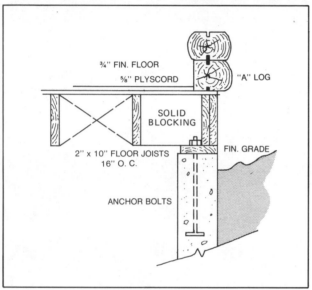

¾" FIN. FLOOR

⅝" PLYSCORD   "A" LOG

SOLID
BLOCKING

2" x 10" FLOOR JOISTS   FIN. GRADE
16" O. C.

ANCHOR BOLTS

Construction details vary with kit homes. Most use a box sill method for subfloor framing, as in this sketch of a typical Vermont Log Building kit home.

You must find your own solution to protecting these materials (see Chapter 9 for some help). The best advice we can give is to get that log house nailed into place as soon as possible. Your vacation home site may seem like the most tranquil spot in the world, but building materials have a habit of "walking" off when left out in the open.

At the time your purchase the kit, the salesperson can probably estimate how long it will take to build it. Although in theory one person can build a small cabin, in reality it takes at least two people. If you can afford it, or can coax friends, four workers are ideal. One kit producer says that with the help of 13 people, a good sized house can be raised in four days.

TOOLS REQUIRED

General carpentry tools are needed for construction of a log house. This includes:

- 6 or 8 lb. sledge hammers—two of them, for driving spikes;
- 3-foot pinch bar—for moving logs and for removing spikes that have been driven in the wrong spots;
- 3-foot level—to check plumb of doors and windows;
- staple gun or staple hammer—for tacking gasket material;
- ratchet winch and 30 feet of rope—for pulling logs tightly together;
- 50- or 100-foot steel tape—for checking various building dimensions;
- a carpenter's claw hammer—for nailing decking, window frames, etc;
- handsaw or power saw—for cutting joists, plywood, etc;
- framing square—for checking square on doors and windows;
- wide-bladed wood chisel—for cleaning mortise cuts;
- drawknife—for trimming logs and removing bark;
- chalk line—for "snapping" lines to align building members.

As logs and other materials are unloaded, they should be separated. Breakables should be put in a safe, dry spot, logs should be sorted by length and use. (Photo Courtesy of Vermont Log Buildings, Inc.)

Some of the tools needed to erect a precut log home.

Other equipment and material that may come in handy includes:

- small chainsaw for cutting larger fireplace opening
- caulking gun
- wire cutters
- electric drill and bits
- flashing for termite shield
- tin snips to cut the flashing
- supply of 2x4's and 1x4's for bracing and framing
- nails (a good supply of 16d and 8d commons, plus a few 20d and 40d)
- conduit (if needed for electric runs)
- hacksaw to cut the conduit
- dunnage or scrap lumber (such as 4x4's) to support the logs off the ground

A chain saw, incidentally, is an excellent investment for virtually every vacation home builder and owner. You can use it while building the house and then to produce firewood later. The log kit supplier you settle on can probably tell you of any exotic tools which might be required.

MATERIALS

Besides the log home kit, you will need other building materials. You will not only need materials for the foundation, but also for the bottom platform and roofing materials. Check these extra requirements out carefully with the log home factory. Usually the salesperson can tell you what extra materials you need to buy. Before you settle on a kit, add the cost of the kit and everything else you will need to buy. That will be the actual cost of the home. Once you get this real cost, you might want to compare it to the cost of a conventionally constructed home to see if indeed it is lower in cost.

As seen in this log cabin during construction, these homes are not difficult to build; however, instructions must be closely followed. (Photo Courtesy of Vermont Log Buildings, Inc.)

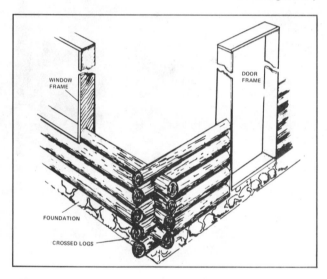

Wilderness Log Home utilizes round logs, with insulation and caulking between logs.

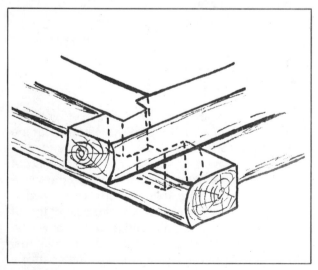

Ward Cabin Company uses squared, white cedar logs with interlocking corners.

ASSEMBLY

Actually, assembling the kit is not difficult, especially if you have enough helpers and a factory representative on hand. Suppliers go to the extreme in labeling kits. Although they are not foolproof, if you follow instructions literally to the letter, you should not have problems.

The first step is to check level and squareness of foundation, and then construct a bottom platform (see Chapter 5). Kit manufacturers will include in-depth instructions on how to construct the bottom platform.

Because each supplier has his own set of instructions, we will only deal in general terms on how a log home is constructed.

THE FIRST COURSE

Usually, before logs are set in place, you have to install a sill seal, usually a type of foam board or other material. This can be stapled into place. Then, with all logs previously separated into piles, you can begin to lay out the first course. It is extremely important to get this first row installed properly because every row you install after it will be influenced by it.

Begin with the front wall of the house and align all logs. When they are in line with the foundation, spike or bolt logs, or otherwise fasten them in place. Usually spikes at the ends of logs are not driven until the adjoining wall log is in place.

With front wall logs in place, the sidewall logs can be added. The sidewalls must sit at right angles to the first wall. An easy way to assure the square of walls is to use the 3,4,5 triangle concept. If you measure out exactly three feet on one wall and four feet on another, the hypotenuse will be exactly five feet. You can also use multiples of the 3,4,5 triangle: 6,8,10 or 9,12,15 for example. With care, the entire first course of logs can be squared and leveled.

DOORS

The doors must be installed next. Read over descriptions of these units to ensure you know inside from outside and top from bottom. Don't laugh. More than a few do-it-yourself log home builders have installed these units improperly.

The doors and frames are installed, leveled and braced. Bracing is usually nothing more than angling an extra 2x4 from the door frame to the platform and temporarily nailing it in place. These braces will hold the doors in place while you fill in around them with logs.

WINDOWS

Next several courses of logs are set and secured according to the manufacturer's instructions. Following instructions closely, you will come to the course where you must add windows. Generally, all the windows are on the same level, and all are added at the same time. Windows and frames are carefully placed on top of the course of logs and then braced. It is not advisable to brace from the side but rather from the top of the frame to the platforms. If you install bracing on the sides of frames, you would then have to move the brace to install logs.

Windows must be treated with the utmost care. The windows should be kept in a closed position to maintain square. Logs should never be forced in around them. If force is necessary, then something is out of square.

FINAL COURSES

With windows in place, log courses around windows are filled in and then longer logs are added over windows. One tip: to prevent a possible twisting of the structure as it is tightened and secured, alternate the tightening of each course; that is, one time tighten it clockwise and then on the next course tighten it counterclockwise.

INSTALLATION DETAILS

JOISTS

In Chapter 5 you will find a section on standard joist installation. You might want to read that over again to reach an understanding of what is involved.

With log homes, you will set a final course and then install ceiling joists. Before installing joists, you will want to check the dimensions of the building to make sure everything is relatively square. If it is somewhat out of square, you can use a come-along to help straighten it out.

A come-along is a rachet winch which comes in handy in construction. It is a device which is attached to one section of the house by use of a metal cable. A longer cable is then fastened to another section. Using a lever and pulleys within the winch, the longer cable is slowly drawn toward the mechanism. If, for example, the framing is slightly out of square, the come-along could be attached to diagonal corners of the framing and then the structure could be slightly drawn in to achieve square. This is a powerful little device. If you have not had experience using it, find someone who knows how to handle it.

The center girder, if called for in the plans, must be installed first. The girder runs at right angles to the ceiling joists and supports them usually at mid span. Sometimes the girder needs the support of a stud wall underneath it. Other times, several 4x4 posts will do the job.

With the girder firmly in place, the joists can now be added. This is a process which will probably take several people due to the weight of the logs. The joists should, however, slip easily into grooves. With joists in place (but not yet spiked or nailed) check for level. You will find that some joists are not level. Most kit manufacturers supply shims which are driven into the grooves at the end of the joist to help level it off. With joists level, and the building in square, you can secure these supports in place.

Depending on plans, more courses of logs can be installed. When joists are secured, you should lay down several sheets of plywood and toenail them into the floor joists so that you have a safe platform on which to work.

PORCH LOGS

Depending on design, porch logs are usually installed now. Some designs have full porches with roofs while others have decks. Porch logs installed on the vertical can be held firmly with braces.

GABLE ENDS

Gable end logs are then installed per your plans. Gable ends should never be left unbraced. They present an easy target for the wind and could either be blown over or knocked out of alignment.

ROOF RAFTERS

Before roof rafters are set in place, the dimensions of the building should again be checked. Once you are sure of the dimensions, toenail in two rafters at a gable end and install the ridge board. The ridge board should be braced with 2x4s to hold it level.

With most kits, the ridge board will come in several sections. The ridge board butt joints should only butt where two roof rafters join—never in the middle of a span.

The rafters should then be installed according to your plans. Start at one end of the house and con-

Interiors of log cabins are very attractive, especially when rough beams are left exposed. (Photo Courtesy of Vermont Log Buildings, Inc.)

tinue to the other. Spike and secure rafters. Remember, any time you temporarily secure any support member, be sure to go back over it and fasten it permanently. Often in the excitment of building, something will be secured only temporarily. This could cause major problems later after construction is complete.

ROOFING

The roof of a log cabin or log home is finished similarly to the roof described in Chapter 5, or according to the log kit plan. Typically, this means that some form of exterior sheathing is applied and then asphalt shingles or wood shakes are applied. Wood shakes make an outstanding roofing material if you can afford them. This material weathers to an attractive color.

FILLING IN

Insulation must be applied under the roof and a vapor barrier must be installed. Insulation can also be used around windows and doors. The unit must also be caulked following kit manufacturer's instructions.

Usually, log home kit builders will leave the logs exposed on the interior. Wood, however, is not as efficient an insulation material as standard insulation. In extremely cold climates you might want to consider using insulation on inside walls and then finishing the wall off in either wallboard or interior paneling.

THE INTERIOR

Once the unit is weathertight, you can begin finishing off the interior. Many log home builders make a big effort to finish the exterior, getting everything weathertight, then finish the inside at a more leisurely pace.

In order of importance, the interior partitions should be completed as soon as possible. Plumbing and electrical should be completed, and then kitchen and bathroom fixtures installed along with fireplace.

This is a quick tour of how to build a log home. As you can see, the construction process is not difficult if you follow plans, and make sure that every course is square and level before beginning the next one.

One final reminder. When you buy a log home kit, you get the structure. But you will need to figure in the cost of labor and other materials to get the total price. If you cost the project out and it is simply too much money, you might want to build a smaller home and then add space later on when you have more money to spend on the project.

7
Kits, Prefabs and Packages

One of the simplest and quickest ways to build the vacation home of your dreams is with a kit, prefab or one of the other packaged homes on the market. In Chapter 6 we described the log cabin, one form of packaged home. Here, we detail factory-built designs more familiar to the average person.

Actually, "manufactured" housing is something of a misnomer because most of the kits available are of standard materials which are cut, hammered, sawn and framed in a similar fashion to conventional construction.

ADVANTAGES

Why build with a kit rather than from scratch? There are a number of good reasons to use a kit. If you are building the house yourself and want something a little out of the ordinary, it will be easier for you to build it with a factory-produced unit. Even if you don't build it yourself, you will have a better understanding of what you are getting and a better handle on costs. Also, professional building talent seems to drop off as you get further away from urban and suburban areas. Show a builder in some far-off place a small but innovative house plan and he is liable to scratch his head and tell you it's going to cost a lot because he's never built anything like that before. Yet a manufactured housing producer will, within several hundred miles of the factory, deliver an entire package and, if you wish, employ an experienced crew to erect it.

You may also complement your own do-it-yourself skills with a factory package; there are generally many building options available. The factory crew can do part of the job or all of it. The less they do, the more you save. While you might not want to put up the rough shell yourself, perhaps you would like to finish the interior for big dollar savings. There are other alternatives: You can complete the foundation and then have the factory crew finish the house, or

vice versa. Usually a program can be created to suit your needs.

Most skilled do-it-yourselfers who have a job and another life away from the vacation home site prefer to have at least the rough shell constructed. This allows them the luxury of completing the remainder of the project when they have the time. This way, even if the house is not completely finished in one season, it is at least protected from the weather.

Another reason to have the shell completed is that you can store other valuable building materials inside. Once a house has been partially constructed, it is vulnerable to theft and vandalism.

CHOOSING THE RIGHT DESIGN

There are many manufacturers of packaged homes on the market today (a partial list is supplied at the end of the book). The largest advertise in national and regional magazines. Because of the regional nature of the business, many good factory-home producers can also be located through local and regional newspapers.

STANDARD STYLES

Manufactured housing can be broken down into five basic categories. These include precut, panelized, prefab, modular and mobile home units. Each type offers certain benefits depending on how much you want to do yourself, how fast you want it done, what you want it to look like, and how much you are willing and able to spend. Here are a few details on each.

Precut. The precut unit is probably the simplest produced in the factory. The manufacturer precuts and prefits every part of the rough shell or finished

Pre-fabricated homes, kits and packages come in many forms, from extremely simple dwellings to high-fashion homes. Here's a precut unit that is as fully compatible with the site as a custom house would be. (Photo courtesy of Acorn Structures)

Although solar energy factory-built houses may or may not be practical for a leisure home (depending on how much you use the unit) they are available. (Photo courtesy of Acorn Structures

house. There are a variety of designs including A-frames, chalets and contemporaries. This package is an excellent choice for a person who wishes to build the unit himself. With all pieces precut and pre-marked, building one of these units is similar to putting together a giant model.

Precut packages come in all price ranges. Large, expensive vacation homes can be had for between $30,000 and $50,000, or more. If budget requirements are strigent, you can get a precut cabin-style vacation unit for only a few thousand dollars—an excellent package for the do-it-yourselfer.

Panelized. Panelized is another form of manufactured housing used extensively for first- and second-home development, as well as for condominiums and apartments. With this type of housing the wall, roof and floor sections are put together on high speed machines. Some large lumber yards offer panelized units for sale. The disadvantage is the limited design choice available through such a manufacturer.

Generally, panelized homes can be erected at a much faster pace than precuts. Usually this is not a good choice for a do-it-yourselfer, because panel fas-

Elements of one precut, factory-built unit: Interlocking laminated decking (1) is nailed to the framework of posts (2) and beams (3) to form the floor and roof system. Exterior walls are installed next between the perimeter panels —consisting of (4) kiln-dried 2x4's and plywood sheathing, glass panels, framed (5) or sliding glass doors (6). Once these panels are in place, asphalt paper (7) and exterior siding (8) are applied. Wall insulation (9), a polyethylene vapor barrier (10) and an interior surface of sheetrock (11) complete exterior walls. Exterior surface of the roof decking is covered with asphalt felt (12), a layer of rigid insulation (13), a second layer of asphalt felt (14) and asphalt roof shingles (15).

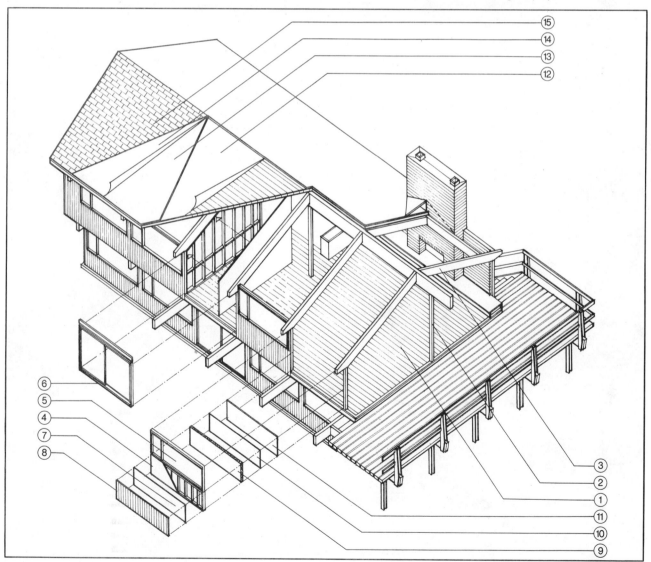

tening techniques require more know-how than the average person possesses.

Prefabricated houses are usually made either in panels or in complete sections, with plumbing and electrical right in the wall. These units are erected on the building site and are ready to live in almost immediately. This is a good choice for someone who wants a vacation house fast, but a poor choice for a do-it-yourselfer seeking to keep costs under control. Only a little money can be saved by making the connections yourself. And these are complicated connections better left to an experienced, certified person.

Here are two factory-built houses being constructed on site. Units have main structural elements constructed, and then side panels and roofing are added. (Photo courtesy of Cluster Shed, Inc.)

Piers which follow the contour of the land can be an economical way to go. Minimal site disturbance was necessary for the construction of this lake front leisure home. (Courtesy of American Plywood Association)

The "Dome Home"

A geodesic dome is an easily constructed and exciting leisure home. There are a variety of kits on the market right for the do-it-yourselfer. (Courtesy of Domes and Homes, Inc.)

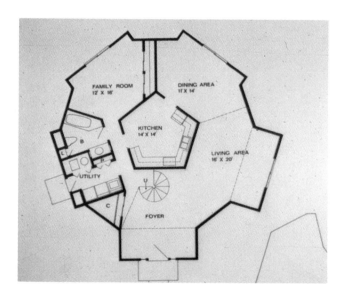

Simple packaged home, built on piles, can offer extra storage space with sheltered patio under which a boat or car can be parked. The design can be suited to any terrain. (Photo courtesy of Jim Walter Homes)

When you want to build it yourself, a log home kit might be the ideal answer. Although there is a wide variety of shapes, sizes and designs available, the most practical for a first-time home builder is a relatively small, one-level unit as shown here. (Courtesy of Vermont Log Cabins)

The hexagon is one of the most space-efficient shapes. This little two-story vacation home in the woods is easily fabricated and versatile enough to offer years of pleasurable living. (Courtesy of Western Wood Products Association)

Basic factory-built houses will give you years of pleasure at an affordable cost. This dwelling is suitable for any environment. (Photo courtesy of Wickes)

Prefabs. Prefabs offer some savings over conventionally built homes. Although there are a variety of designs available, they are not as extensive as that found with precut or panelized units. Prices range between $10,000 to $15,000, and up. These units originally had a reputation for being produced for the bottom of the housing market, but today their image has improved. The prime benefit of a prefab is that you can have a fully erected vacation home in a few days or weeks, rather than months.

Modular. Modular homes have gained prominence in recent years. These units differ from prefabs in that they are usually bigger, and arrive at the house site more or less complete. They also provide cost-savings over conventionally built homes.

Because of highway laws, the units must be no more than 14 feet wide and no more than 64 feet long. Although design options are more limited than with other types of manufactured homes, variations are available. These units are not for the do-it-yourselfer, but for people who want a vacation home fast and at relatively low cost.

Mobile homes. Mobile homes are really a type of modular housing. If you have never thought of a mobile home as a viable vacation home alternative, check into it. Mobile homes are not trailers anymore. In fact, there are some designs which, once set in place, appear to be conventional housing.

Mobile homes go in place fast. Although they are limited by highway laws, there are double-wide and triple-wide units available. That is, the house will be delivered at the construction site in two or three different units which are then connected together side-by-side to form a big house.

There are problems with mobile homes. Some jurisdictions will not permit their use. These are archaic rules which sought to zone out this form of housing when it consisted of little more than a trailer sitting on a cinderblock base. One other problem is that many lending institutions will not give conventional financing for a mobile home. Instead, they will give you financing similar to an auto loan—high-interest short-term arrangement.

FINDING A FACTORY

Selecting a manufactured home is no easy task. There are many producers and it is difficult to tell one from another.

Thankfully, there is a process of elimination to help you narrow the choice. For any particular vacation home site, there are only a limited number of factories which can service the area. Some mobile home factories deal on a national basis, but most other types of factories deal on a regional basis—perhaps a radius of 500 or 600 miles from the factory. Your choice will be further limited to those units within your price range and design tastes.

Select the house you want from a model, not from literature. That's the only way you can tell if the house is right for your needs. If a local dealer does not have the model you are thinking of purchasing, visit the factory; it will usually have a larger selection of models available.

Be sure you receive answers to all of your questions. The most important is, how much will the completed house cost. If the factory cannot give you a firm price, then consult the local contractor in your area who would have the job of constructing it. You may be bowled over by a lovely model home which has a package price of $15,000. Unfortunately, that $15,000 package may cost another $20,000 once it has been constructed on your site. Another point you must clarify before you go into contract is the shipping charge. Some factories will quote you a price for a unit, but will add on a substantial shipping charge.

Delivery date is another sticky problem. If you order a house on June 15th, don't expect it complete and ready to move into by July 4th. Although the package does not take long to produce or to erect, once the building season gets going there may be a long wait. Your best bet is to order the package during late autumn or winter if you want it ready by early spring.

CONSTRUCTION NOTES

SITE ACCESS

One other factor you must consider in addition to design is the site. If it is five miles back on a narrow dirt road, the large 18-wheel truck carrying your new home may not be able to negotiate the road. Therefore, truck access to the site becomes important.

The best type of site for a factory-built housing unit is one in which a truck can drive right up to the site, and where material can be unloaded next to the foundation. If you have to haul materials even a short distance, it can greatly add to labor costs and the time it takes to build the unit.

This is usually not a problem in a developed second-home area such as a beach, lake or mountain resort. It does become a severe problem in less-developed areas. If you are ordering a precut cabin from a manufacturer, the materials can probably be transported on a jeep or pickup truck from the drop-off point to the building site. Larger packages are too unwieldy for that.

TIME SAVER

In Chapter 5 you can read about constructing a house from scratch. With factory precuts and some prefabs the process is basically the same but with one important difference: Each structural member that must be calculated and cut is instead ready to go.

INTERIOR FINISHES

For interior finishes, some factory home producers will give you the option of purchasing the materials of your choice for interior finish at wholesale plus 10 percent. Others will rely on their dealers to help you with this. Others leave the problem of finishing the interior totally up to you.

BUILDING BLOCKS

One variation on the concept of designing your own home is literally putting building modules together to create a serviceable home. One New Hampshire manufacturer has come up with a system that comprises three elements: a 12 foot by 12 foot module, a 9 foot by 12 foot porch that can be enclosed, and a deck. The module features 12 foot sliding glass doors, and a transparent plexiglass story. The module, a shell of post and beam framing with a shed roof, costs approximately $2,500, while the module plus one deck would cost under $3,000.

By coupling modules, porches and decks you can have a "customized" design for a fairly modest price. One-, two- and three-bedroom designs can be created, with space ranging from 450 square feet to more than 1,100 square feet. As usual, prices do not include insulation, partitions, interior finishes or fixtures.

This type of system is geared for amateur builders. The manufacturer provides all of the tools needed for construction and suggests that kits for two or three modules with deck/porch can be loaded on one 16-foot truck.

Many factory producers give you a wide choice of units, some are infinitely expandable. This small unit by itself with a deck could be an adequate and affordable vacation home. As can be seen by the accompanying diagram, separate areas are provided for basic functions: kitchen, dining, living, sleeping and storge. (Art courtesy of Shelter-Kit, Inc.)

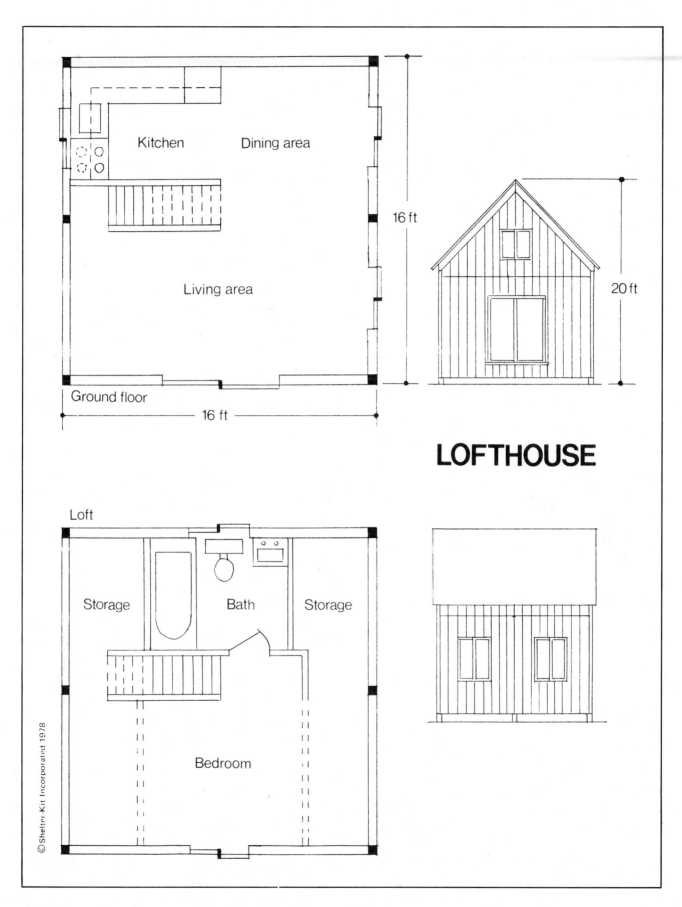

Kitchen

Dining area

Living area

16 ft

Ground floor

16 ft

20 ft

LOFTHOUSE

Loft

Storage

Bath

Storage

Bedroom

© Shelter-Kit Incorporated 1978

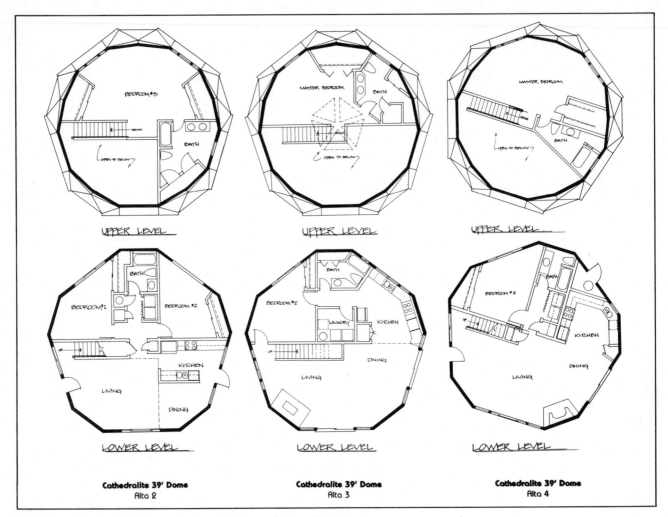

Domes make excellent homes. Here are three floor plans which show living space available. (Courtesy of Cathedralite Domes)

UNUSUAL SHAPES

For the adventurous, a cabin or an A-frame or a conventional rectangular-shaped home might not be satisfactory. The geodesic dome (described in Chapter 2) is one answer; the hexagon is another.

Like the dome design, a hexagon offers great interior design flexibility because none of the walls are loadbearing. And since these packages are generally put together with nuts, bolts and screws, sections can be added or disassembled for a change in design. As with domes, too, the triangle is the basic structural element.

Tools needed include: wrench, drill with attachment for self-tapping screws, caulking gun, and ordinary carpenter tools.

A hexagon-shaped home of 700 square feet features about 30 feet covered with walls, for a net living space of 670 square feet. A rectangular-shaped home of 32 feet by 22 feet, or 704 square feet, features 141 square feet covered with walls, for a net living space of 563 square feet.

While erection cost of the basic structure may be low, ranging from under $3,000 for a basic 704-square-foot home to under $10,000 for a 2,800-square-foot version, that cost is just a fraction of the total cost. Total cost would include freight (several hundred dollars), plumbing, heating and air conditioning, wiring, landscaping, and site preparation. The total cost, in fact, could range anywhere from three to nearly 10 times the basic erection cost.

SOLAR HOMES

Solar systems for domestic hot water and space heating are the new frontier in residential energy conservation technology, and if you wish to be a solar pioneer you may choose this type of packaged home.

One manufacturer offers a "Cape" design with a 47 degree roof pitch, on the belief that roof collectors should not monopolize the southern exposure and view. Solar garages are another alternative. This solar system is designed to provide between 40 percent and 70 percent of the home's heating needs; a back-up system such as an oil-fired warm air furnace is needed.

These Capes have been designed so that overhangs shade the glass when the sun is high in the summer, but let the sun's heat into the living space during winter. Sun-warmed air is distributed throughout the rest of the house by heating system return ducts.

Solar systems work best in homes that are properly insulated to cut down on heat loss through walls, roof and floors. Standard construction of these Capes includes double insulated glass, weatherstripping, minimum windows on the northern exposure, internal chimneys, maximum insulation in walls, roof and floors, and entries designed to cut down on the amount of cold air coming into the home.

But if you select a packaged home with a solar heating system, be prepared for the expense. Solar systems generally will add at least 10 percent to the cost. That's because the technology is not advanced enough, or the units produced in sufficient quantity, to lower the costs of the main components.

So, you can figure on a cost of approximately $40,000 to $50,000 for the shell of a solar "Cape," which includes a weathertight structure on foundation, studded partitions, stairs, decks and kitchen cabinets. The finished home, however, excluding the cost of the solar system, would be between $70,000 to $80,000 and up.

8
Energy-saving Tips

Energy conservation is important everywhere. But in vacation homes, it may or may not be of concern depending on the scope of the project, the number of seasons in use, and climate. Small cabins used only on a warm summer weekend really do not need a lot of energy-saving features because very little energy is consumed (although there are ways, detailed in this chapter, to make small cabins more comfortable in hot weather). Large vacation homes used in all four seasons should have as many energy-saving features as primary homes.

Although it would take an entire volume or more to detail everything you need to know about energy conservation, in this chapter we will touch on the most crucial elements. Also, check Appendix C for addresses of companies that make wind-power products, solar devices, and skylights.

INSULATION

Without question, the best barrier between you and high energy bills is insulation. It's the most important energy-saver you can install in the house. And even if you are just contemplating a weekend cabin, remember that if you decide to sell it sometime in the future, well-insulated walls, floors and ceilings will bring a higher price.

Insulation works most efficiently when it is applied to every area which is in contact with the exterior. This barrier keeps hot or cold air outside and reduces the amount of draft. All insulation works the same way; it reduces the amount of heat transferred from a warm area to a cold area. When selecting insulation, the material with the highest "R" value (resistance to heat flow) gives you the lowest transfer of heat. But

Different types of insulation give different "R" values. The greater the thickness of insulation the more resistance to heat flow you will achieve (Dept. of Housing and Urban Development)

TYPE OF INSULATION

	BATTS OR BLANKETS		LOOSE FILL (POURED-IN)			
	glass fiber	rock wool	glass fiber	rock wool	cellulosic fiber	
R-11	3½"-4"	3"	5"	4"	3"	R-11
R-19	6"-6½"	5¼"	8"-9"	6"-7"	5"	R-19
R-22	6½"	6"	10"	7"-8"	6"	R-22
R-30	9½"-10½"*	9"*	13"-14"	10"-11"	8"	R-30
R-38	12"-13"*	10½"*	17"-18"	13"-14"	10"-11"	R-38

* two batts or blankets required.

today, there are other criteria which also must be taken into account when specifying insulation.

CHOICES

There are many different types of insulation on the market. These include mineral fiber, cellulosic fiber, foamed plastics and expanded mineral materials.

Mineral fiber. On the market for many years, this is one of the oldest forms of "modern" insulation. Originally, it was manufactured by melting down slag, a by-product of steel production. Today, the product is either rock wool or fiberglass, and comes in batts or blankets. It is an extremely effective type of insulation which can be used by the do-it-yourselfer in walls, crawl spaces and ceilings.

The material is fireproof; however, the vapor barriers attached to the insulation are not. Normally it can be purchased with or without paper vapor barriers. (Vapor barriers are generally a paper or plastic material used to reduce the movement of moisture from a warm to a cold area. They are an essential part of a good insulation job, preventing moisture buildup in walls and attic areas.)

Cellulosic fiber. Produced from wood pulp or another wood fiber material such as old newspapers, the material is not fireproof in itself; a fire retardant material must be added. Some of the fire retardants added cause damage to piping and heating ducts in the wall due to chemical corrosion. This is not an indictment of the material, because there are many fine products available which will serve you well for many years. The Federal Trade Commission, however, has received a number of consumer complaints about some brands of this insulation, and is apparently probing the industry.

Cellulosic fiber insulation produced by a legitimate manufacturer is a good product. But when shortages of insulation cropped up in recent years, some people started producing and selling this type of insulation without taking any steps to make it safe for use. In some cases, this type of insulation was sold in "plain brown paper bags" without label. If purchasing this type of insulation, check that it is properly labeled, with fire retardant chemicals listed.

Foamed plastics. These include polyurethane, polystyrene or urea formaldehyde. Often, this substance is used as packaging material for delicate items such as high fidelity components. Typically, it is molded around the product and holds it firmly in its box. Foamed plastics offer the benefit of a very high "R" value. This insulation usually comes in boards, and is easy to install. However, it can never be used without use of a fireproof wall covering such as gypsum wallboard. Although this material is fire-resistant, when exposed to extremely high temperatures it can melt and produce a dangerous, toxic smoke.

Expanded mineral materials. This insulation includes substances such as vermiculite and perlite. Expanded mineral materials are definitely fireproof. But because of the nature of the material, it must be blown or dumped into place. Many contractors are available with machinery to blow this insulation in place. But if you want to insulate your own house, about the only place you can use this material is in the attic. And then you must dump bags of the granule material between ceiling joists.

HOW & WHERE TO INSULATE

If you are going to do the job yourself, we will assume that either you built the house yourself (see Chapter 5) or you had a builder erect a rough shell. Rough plumbing and rough electrical should already be installed and systems should have been tested before insulating begins.

Heat rises; therefore, the most crucial place to insulate is in the ceiling or attic. If you do not intend to use the attic for anything else, it is easiest to place the insulation between ceiling joists. If the attic is large enough and if you plan to finish it off someday, the most practical place to insulate is between roof rafters.

In either case there are a number of things you must do before insulating. First, check to make sure you have adequate ventilation in the space (see section in this chapter). Mark the ventilators, and do *not* cover them with insulation. Next, locate all light fixtures. Often "bullet type" light fixtures are installed in ceilings and penetrate into the attic space. In no case should you insulate around these light fixtures. Whether you will use loose fill or a blanket type insulation, build a simple wooden frame around the light fixture to keep insulation away from it. The sides of the box should be the same depth as the insulation you wish to install. In this situation, it's not only the insulation which could be a problem, but the light fixture itself. Fiberglass insulation won't burn, but it is such a good insulation that if it were packed around a fixture it might cause the fixture to overheat.

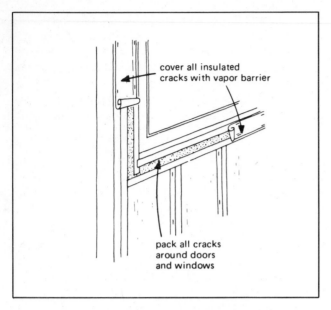

For a thorough insulation job, it is necessary to not only fill wall and floor cavities but also small spaces such as those between window frame and wall. (Art courtesy of National Mineral Wool Insulation Assn.)

Sideview of typical wall. Note that the vapor barrier, whether it attached to the insulation or completely separate, always faces the warm side of the structure. This enables the insulation and structure of the building to remain dry.

Next, check the attic space to ensure that there are no leaks. Wet insulation is bad insulation. Therefore, check and correct problems.

Now you need to think about a vapor barrier for your insulation. Vapor barriers, regardless of type, always face toward the warm part of the house. That is, if you are installing insulation between ceiling joists, the vapor barrier goes down first. If you are insulating roof rafters, the vapor barrier faces in toward the attic space.

The most convenient insulation to install is batt or blanket insulation with a vapor barrier already attached. If, for instance, you have 8″ ceiling joists in your attic, you can use either 6″ or 8″ insulation and roll or place it between joists with the vapor barrier facing down. That's all there is to the job.

If you choose to use insulation without a paper vapor barrier, you will have to install a vapor barrier before you apply insulation. The best product to use in this case is plastic sheeting. To insulate between roof rafters, you will have to roll out the vapor barrier and insulation and as you do so you will have to staple the lip of it to the roof rafter. Insulation should be stapled from the lowest point of the rafters on up to the peak of the roof. As mentioned, the vapor barrier should be visible to you when the job is done.

The sidewalls of the attic must also be insulated. Here, insulation is again rolled out and stapled in place. Remember do not cover up any vents.

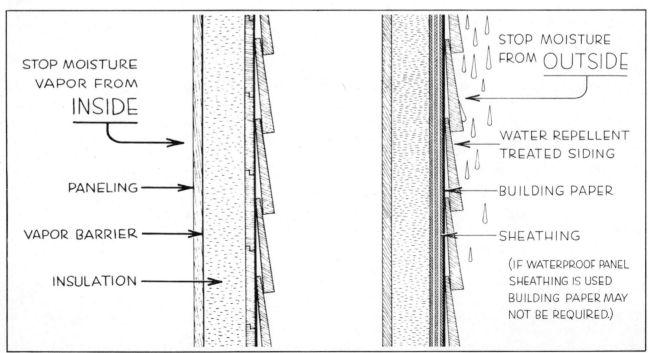

Also, any time you use insulation material, you should wear a mask or some other type of breathing apparatus. These materials often break off and become airborne when being pushed and shoved around. Many of the materials may bother you.

For walls, use batts or blankets if you intend to do the job yourself. Again, purchase insulation with vapor barriers. Then staple insulation into place with the vapor barrier facing in toward the warm section of the house. When the job is done, you should be able to see rows upon rows of silver vapor barriers. Insulation should be stapled from the lowest part of the floor right up to the high point in the wall. All exterior walls should have insulation for best results.

When you come upon oddly spaced sections of the wall which will not take the full blanket of insulation, rip off a portion and simply stuff it in place. All spaces around windows and doors should have insulation stuffed in before the final wall covering is added.

Remember, to the greatest extent possible, you want to seal off the interior of your house from the weather outside. The only way to do that is to staple or stuff insulation in every exterior wall or space.

As you go along, you may come upon plumbing and heating ducts in the wall if you have constructed an extensive vacation home. Where possible, insulate behind pipes and heating ducts to protect them from the exterior. In no case should they run through an uninsulated area. If you cannot stuff insulation be-

hind, then wrap pipes and ducts in special insulation you can buy for that purpose. For pipes in particular, it is not just a matter of energy conservation but protecting the pipe itself from freezing and bursting. More than one vacation home owner has had the unfortunate experience of arriving at his or her favorite retreat only to find water spewing all over walls, floor and furniture.

Basements present another problem and another opportunity for energy saving. If your house has a full foundation with masonry walls or if it has a crawl space with masonry walls and no insulation either on the walls or between floor joists, it is an uninsulated area. Masonry walls look as though they should have insulation value, but they do not.

Let's tackle full foundations first. You can frame out the basement walls with 2x4 studs and then staple insulation between wall cavities. That requires a lot of materials and a lot of work. Or you can nail 1x2 furring strips to the walls with masonry nails and apply board insulation over the furring strips. If you opt for this method, the furring strips should be applied 24 inches on center if you are using 24-inch-wide boards. Then the walls must be covered with wallboard.

Unless you plan on using the basement as living space, the easiest and least expensive way to insulate is to apply the material in the cavities between floor joists. Stapling does not work well in this situation because gravity tends to pull insulation down after a

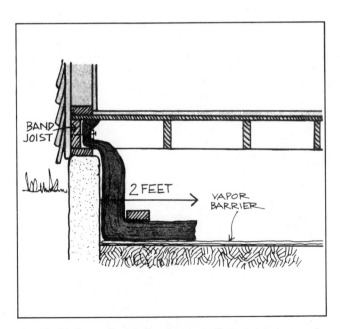

An alternative to insulating between floor joists in crawl space construction is to lay insulation on sidewall and ground. (Dept. of Housing and Urban Development)

When insulating under house, material can be stapled in place and then wire can be strung to hold it firmly in place. (Art courtesy of National Mineral Wool Insulation Assn.)

while. An extremely effective way to insulate here is to apply the insulation and then staple a wire mesh to joists to hold it securely in place. Vapor barriers should be directed toward the warm area of the house.

If your home is slab on grade, there is still something you can do to reduce energy bills. Before the house is backfilled, apply board insulation against the outside foundation wall down to about the same depth as the frost line. No special connections are needed. Simply lay the insulation on its side and then apply earth behind it to hold in place.

In a vacation home situation, many have the home constructed on a crawl space. There might be either a crawl space constructed of masonry block or a crawl space created through pier construction. Insulation can be applied between floor joists in a similar fashion as in a full foundation. Another option is to lay insulation against the crawl space side walls. In either case, face the vapor barrier toward the warm part of the house. It is also advisable to lay a plastic sheet on the bare earth under the crawl space to help keep moisture under control.

WINDOWS AND DOORS

WINDOWS

Windows and doors are critical when energy conservation is a prime goal. But as mentioned previously, if you intend to use the house only in the summer, these areas are not critical.

Windows use up energy in several ways. First, air often infiltrates around panes of glass and the window frame causing drafts and a waste of energy. Secondly, glass is an excellent conductor of heat. It conducts heat out of the house in winter and into the house in summer. Windows also transfer heat through radiation. When the sun shines in during the summer it can heat the place up. When it shines in during winter, it helps to keep the space warm. (See section in Chapter 2 on window placement.)

Windows with wooden frames conduct less heat than those with aluminum frames. However, the wood units cost considerably more. Before you decide which to buy, measure the potential cost savings against the first cost of windows.

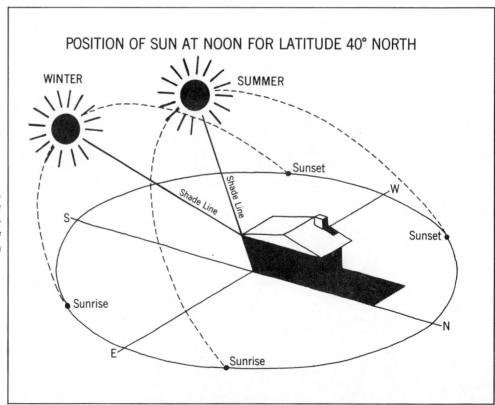

Windows located on the south side of the house will be in full sun in winter but not in summer. (Dept. of Agriculture)

POSITION OF SUN AT NOON FOR LATITUDE 40° NORTH

WINTER SUMMER Sunset Shade Line Shade Line W Sunset S Sunrise N E Sunrise

Double-insulated glass is an extremely good energy saver. If you intend to use the vacation house in summer only, it may not be worthwhile to invest in this; however, extensive use of the house in winter may require it.

Big windows use up more energy than small ones. How you will use your vacation house will influence this. If you plan to be at your retreat in the cold of winter, smaller windows will help keep the place cozier.

Storm windows are really necessary for regular winter use. If you choose not to spend the extra money on storms, you can still save energy by installing do-it-yourself storm windows made of clear plastic and held in place with strips of quarter round molding. The only drawback to this type of quick storm window is that it will consume a lot of your weekend to cut and fasten them in place.

DOORS

The real energy saver for doors and movable sections of windows is weatherstripping. Weatherstripping is made of either metal, plastic or felt strips, and is designed to seal between the movable sections of windows and doors and thus cut down on energy waste and cold drafts. Metal weatherstripping holds up best and is most expensive; felt is the cheapest. Unless you want to apply weatherstripping every year or two, go with the metal.

There are a variety of insulated doors on the market. Usually they have metal faces with insulation sandwiched in between. The ordinary wood door offers some insulation but not nearly as much as a well-insulated wall.

Storm doors will make a wood door more efficient. An excellent choice here is to buy a combination storm and screen door. That way you'll keep the cold out in the winter and the bugs out in summer.

CAULKING

Caulking is a material which reduces those hidden energy wasters: all the cracks in siding and between window and door frames. Caulking is necessary not only to keep out cold drafts, but also water.

Caulking comes in disposable cartridges and is applied with the aid of a caulking gun. Three types are available, including: oil or resin base; latex, butyl or polyvinyl base; or, elastomeric.

Oil- or resin-base caulk will bond to almost any surface. It is not very durable, but is cheapest. The latex, butyl or polyvinyl caulk will bond to most surfaces. It lasts longer and is more expensive. The elastomeric caulks are the most durable and the most expensive. Unless you want to spend a lot of time working around your vacation home, spend the extra dollars for the elastomeric.

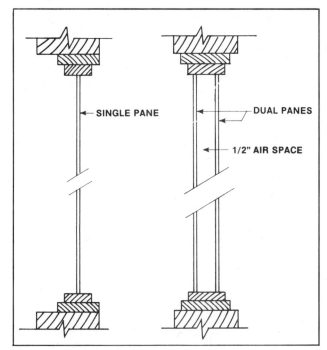

If you use double-glazed glass you can usually reduce heat loss by about 50% (Art courtesy of Owens-Corning Fiberglas)

An inexpensive way to construct energy-saving storm windows is to purchase a roll of clear plastic and then secure it to window frames with strips of molding. (Dept. of Housing and Urban Development)

HEATING AND COOLING SYSTEMS

Depending on the scope of your vacation home, you may or may not install a central heating system. These systems are expensive and unless you use your house frequently in cold weather, don't bother with one.

If you opt for one, carefully check the price and availability of fuel in the vacation home area. Although natural gas may be available and relatively inexpensive, it may be too costly to lay pipe for it from a supply to your house. In many vacation home areas bottled gas is available, but this is usually a very expensive way to heat a home.

Oil is another possibility but make sure that an oil delivery truck can negotiate your road. This will require another excavation on your building site for the oil tank.

Electricity is very expensive but it just might be necessary if you need winter heating. Its only virtue is that it is easy and relatively inexpensive to install on a first-cost basis. Used extensively over the years, however, this first cost savings will disappear.

If you use your house only infrequently over the winter, you might want to invest in several good electric resistance heaters. While most people interested in energy conservation would balk at using such devices, they will heat up a cold house. And if you use them only occasionally, the bill won't be that great.

FIREPLACE HEAT

For many vacation home users, a central heating system is not needed because the house is only used in spring, summer and autumn. Basically, these people need something to take the chill out of the air in the early morning and evening. In most climates, a well-functioning fireplace could achieve this.

The typical fireplace, however, does not operate at great efficiency. In fact, most operate at no more than 15 percent efficiency. That means for every log you burn, you only derive about 15 percent of the potential heating power. But there's more bad news. Besides having low efficiency, most fireplaces have extremely efficient flues. An effective flue will not only remove smoke from the fire, but a good portion of the already-heated air in the room.

Fireplaces can be made more efficient. The flue, for instance, should always be closed when the unit is not in use. A good airtight cover will keep much of the air in the room while the fireplace is in operation. There are also a number of different grates on the market which enable more heat to move into the living space.

There are a number of heat circulating fireplaces on the market today that can greatly increase efficiency. This unit by Heatilator is installed by (1) cutting a hole in ceiling and roof; (2) installing insulated pipe; (3) framing out metal unit with 2x4 studs, and (4) covering framing with plywood and choice of covering such as paneling or simulated brick or stone.

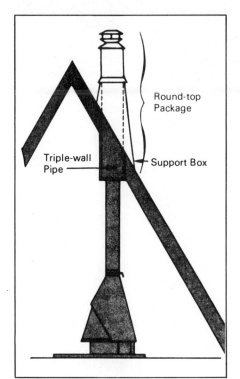

A-frame roofs pose no installation problems with the proper chimney package.

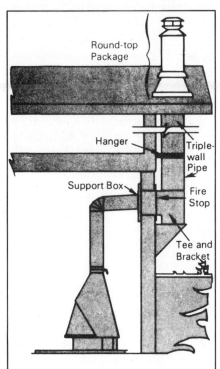

No need to cut through the attic. It's easy to elbow through an outside wall and vent straight up, using Tee and Bracket.

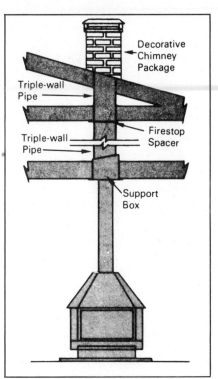

First floor installation in a two-story house. Chimney can be concealed in a second story closet.

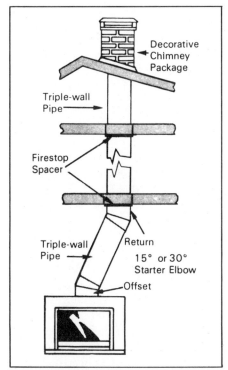

Preway chimneys clear upstairs obstructions with 15° or 30° elbows (all elbow kits include offset and return).

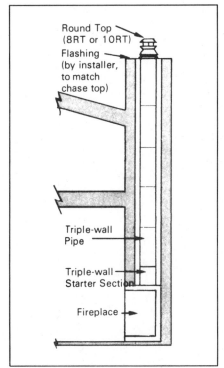

Today's space saving chase installations are a natural with Preway built-in fireplaces and chimney system.

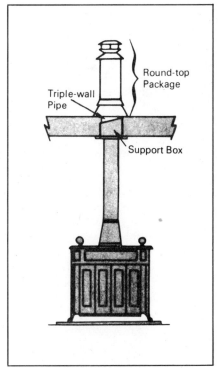

Installation through a flat roof is simple and the most economical of all.

Fireplaces and wood burning stoves can be installed in a variety of ways. Shown here are six different chimney installations. (Art courtesy of Preway)

When constructing a masonry fireplace in a new vacation home, plan to have the main section of the chimney run up through the interior of the house rather than up an exterior wall. This is a great energy saver. The masonry walls will heat up over the course of an evening while the fire is burning. Then later as the house begins to cool down, the masonry walls will give up heat and help keep the house warm. If masonry walls were outside of the house, heat would be almost immediately lost to the out of doors.

Vacation home owners generally do not have as much money to spend on their second home as they do on their first. Therefore, a free-standing metal fireplace might be selected over a masonry unit. Many of the same techniques of energy saving apply to the free-standing unit.

Free-standing fireplaces can be installed by a do-it-yourselfer. The only real difficult part is the required hole in the roof. You may wish to hire a carpenter for a few hours to cut the hole. Other than that, the unit can be simply installed by following manufacturer's instructions.

WOOD-BURNING STOVES

As a source of extra heat, a good, solid wood-burning stove should be selected over a fireplace. Although they are not as elegant or as beautiful as a fireplace, they do put out considerably more heat. You must decide which is more important to you.

A good wood-burning stove is more efficient for several reasons. First, it draws less heat out of the room when its doors are shut. Usually, it will draw just enough air for combustion and little more. As the logs burn, the metal mass of the unit heats up and through conduction and convection it gives off considerable heat.

There are old-fashioned wood-burning stoves called Franklin stoves that are efficient and beautiful. A good unit will cost several hundred dollars, but is well worth it in terms of the years of performance it will give you. Some are available for a lot less. But if there is one item in your new vacation home that you should not skimp on, it's the wood-burning stove.

Sometimes you will find these units available in an out-of-the way antique or thrift shop. Be careful what you buy, particularly if it is a "bargain." Until several years ago a very good and lovely old stove could be purchased this way. But today, those people living in that out-of-the-way place need additional heat just as much as you do. If a stove is available at a bargain, it's probably no good. The authors sought to purchase a stove this way and had no luck. On inspection, the

bargains had considerable rust and in some cases were rusted out. Others had cracks in the weld seam. Whether you buy a unit new or used, you should look closely at all seams. A welding that is rough, pocked or cracked means that the unit was either constructed poorly or was damaged. Over the years, all a crack can do is grow larger.

Our advice is to purchase a wood-burning stove from a reputable dealer. Purchase the unit new and do not be afraid to pay a good price for it. When buying the unit, be sure that delivery is included in the price. A good stove weighs hundreds of pounds and is difficult to handle. It might also be a good idea to get the dealer to install the unit for you. If you decide to do it yourself, make sure the unit comes with in-depth instructions.

There's another option in wood-burning stoves. You can build one yourself. There are kits on the market today which allow you to make a wood-burning stove out of a 55-gallon steel drum. Although you can make a functioning stove this way, the steel is not a particularly heavy gauge. Further, this type of unit does not look nearly as good as a Franklin stove. In fact, once it is set up, it looks like a 55-gallon drum you converted into a stove—nothing more, nothing less.

There's also a word of caution in converting a steel drum. Make sure you thoroughly wash it out before you try to saw it apart or cut it with a welding torch. If it contains any residue of a combustible fluid, you might be in for a tragic surprise.

WATER HEATERS

You might not want central heating, but you will want a hot water heater. You can go with a standard hot water heater or you might want to install a solar hot water heater. Although solar heating systems are not really practical for a vacation home, a solar hot water heater could be.

If you want a standard hot water heater, you can select between a 30-gallon and 50-gallon tank. Most first homes have about a 50-gallon tank. If you think hot water usage will be less at your vacation home, you might want to select the smaller size.

For a vacation home owner, the biggest savings from a hot water heater comes with *remembering* to shut the unit off between visits to the house. If you are just there on weekends, keeping your hot water heater on all week will boost your bills to wasteful proportions.

For year around use, you can insulate your hot water heater. There are kits available for relatively lit-

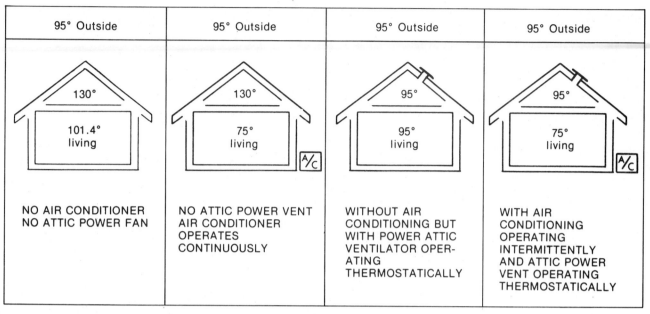

95° Outside	95° Outside	95° Outside	95° Outside
130°	130°	95°	95°
101.4° living	75° living	95° living	75° living
NO AIR CONDITIONER NO ATTIC POWER FAN	NO ATTIC POWER VENT AIR CONDITIONER OPERATES CONTINUOUSLY	WITHOUT AIR CONDITIONING BUT WITH POWER ATTIC VENTILATOR OPER- ATING THERMOSTATICALLY	WITH AIR CONDITIONING OPERATING INTERMITTENTLY AND ATTIC POWER VENT OPERATING THERMOSTATICALLY

A properly ventilated attic will greatly reduce temperatures in the living space below. (Art courtesy of Leslie-Locke)

tle cost. Basically what you do is add another layer of insulation to the outside of the unit.

Insulating hot water pipes always saves energy, whether you use the house all year around or just in the summer. This can be quickly accomplished by purchasing rolls of insulating tape which are wrapped around hot water pipes.

Another big saver of hot water is to install a cold water shower outside of your vacation home. That way, people coming back from the beach, lake or pool can rinse themselves off there rather than wasting hot water. A shower can be built very inexpensively particularly if it's just a rinse-off unit. A garden hose can be connected to a water source inside the house and directed outside. You can either bury it or leave it on the ground. Then a piece of lumber— perhaps a 4x4—can be set in the ground. The hose can be attached to it along with a shower head, and a means to turn it on and off. For only a few dollars, you have an outside shower. If you need to build a shower stall for the unit, you can do so by making a three-sided box out of plywood panels and then adding a shower curtain for the fourth side.

VENTILATION

Good ventilation, particularly in the attic, not only contributes to lower energy bills but a more comfort-

able environment as well. Even if energy conservation is not a major concern in your project, comfort should be. On a hot summer's day when it's around 100 degrees in your living room, it could reach 130 degrees in an unventilated attic. What's worse, at night when it cools down outside, that trapped heat radiates into the living space of your house and keeps everything uncomfortably warm. Further, if hot air can be trapped in the attic, water vapor can as well. If moisture is allowed to remain in the area over a long period of time, dry rot will develop.

The solution is fortunately simple: Add ventilation. Probably the fastest way to do it is to install a power ventilator. This costs money to operate but it changes the stale air quickly and efficiently.

Static ventilators, however, are usually adequate for most climates. These units are built right into the structure and replace hot or stale air slowly but efficiently.

VENTS

Usually, a combination of static vents offers the best service.

Roof louvers. These are small domes located near the ridge of the roof. They come in aluminum, steel or plastic. You can buy them with or without screens.

Several types of roof vents are available to maintain air flow and proper ventilation in attic. (Art courtesy of H.C. Products)

The units with screens block air flow slightly, but they do keep insects out of the space.

Turbine wheel.   This is really a variation of a roof louver. The unit comes with a wheel or turbine which turns in the wind and draws air out of the attic. In severe weather, rain can penetrate through both the turbine wheel and the roof louver.

Gable-end louvers.   These simple units are triangular or rectangular and as the name implies are placed at the end of the house. These work most efficiently when the wind blows through them.

Ridge vents.   This is a long vent which provides continuous circulation of air along the ridge of the house.

Soffit vents.   This vent offers air flow along the floor of the attic.

Probably the best combination of vents is ridge vent in conjunction with soffit vent. This is a good combination because there are vents at the highest point and lowest point of the space.

Ventilation in other areas of the house should be considered during design. The simplest way to achieve good ventilation in the living space is to have windows and doors on opposite walls which can be opened to allow cross-ventilation.

You might also consider a small fan in the kitchen and bathroom to help remove moisture from the house. In vacation homes, space is often at a premium, which results in a small kitchen and bathroom. If these areas are so designed that good natural ventilation is not possible, a small exhaust fan is definitely recommended.

GOOD MAINTENANCE

A key energy-saver in vacation homes as well as your primary home is regular maintenance. For instance, empty your hot water heater and drain sludge out at least once a year. Often, foreign matter in drinking water will collect in the hot water tank. This acts as an insulator at the bottom of the tank and reduces the efficiency of the unit.

Maintenance of water faucets should also be routine. A faucet which continually drips will not only waste water, but over a season it will cost you plenty in higher bills.

Weatherstripping and caulking should also be checked at least once a year. Material which is damaged or worn out should be replaced.

Depending on the scope of your home, heating systems should be regularly maintained and balanced. Although yearly maintenance is not crucial for a natural gas system, an oil burner is a different matter. As in an automobile, an out-of tune oil burner will greatly increase your fuel costs.

9
Space Savers & Maintenance

PLANNING A SMALL KITCHEN

A kitchen is more than just a place to prepare and cook food. In vacation homes the kitchen is likely to also serve as a center of activity and entertainment. To create a small kitchen where spending time is a pleasure, not a chore, the key elements are: appliance layout, cabinets and other storage space, countertop work space, lighting, and dining areas or counters.

Kitchen appliance manufacturers and cabinet designers have carried out considerable research to discover the most efficient appliance layouts. The results show that food preparation, cooking, and cleaning tasks take place within what is known as a "work triangle." This triangle can be roughly drawn from the refrigerator to the rangetop to the sink. If the sides of the imaginary triangle are equal, the kitchen will be quite efficient. For maximum efficiency, the sides of that triangle should be about 16 feet, though a smaller triangle would also prove workable.

For efficient arrangment of appliances, cabinets and countertops, there are L- and U-shaped kitchens. Single-bowl sinks take up less space than double-bowl sinks, and cost less.

Wall cabinets, pantries and base cabinets come in a standard 12-inch depth that can provide a lot of storage space. If you analyze your family needs (i.e., do you rely a lot on canned or boxed food; do you have a large supply and variety of dishes and glassware; will you be using a food processor and other small appliances?) you can plan storage space accordingly.

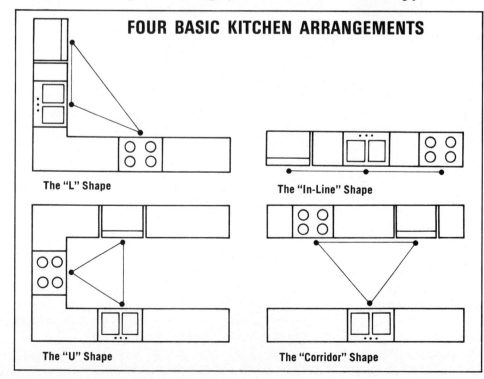

FOUR BASIC KITCHEN ARRANGEMENTS

The "L" Shape

The "In-Line" Shape

The "U" Shape

The "Corridor" Shape

Shown are the four basic kitchen arrangements. In small spaces, U-shapes and In-line shapes are most workable. (Art courtesy of Haas Cabinets, Inc.)

The interior of this vacation home is kept simple with the kitchen installed along one wall and an open area for dining and seating. Window seating is one way of maximizing use of interior space. (Photo courtesy of McCue, Boone, Tomsick Architects)

Storage space in standard cabinets can be greatly increased with a little ready-made hardware: lazy susans, plastic dish and utensil racks, adjustable shelves made of a variety of materials including plastic bins, vinyl-covered steel rods, and plywood. Utility cabinets of 83½ inch height are useful to store mops, brooms and other items.

Use the space above wall cabinets for storage of baskets or serving trays. The space under the wall cabinets can be used for narrow shelves that hold spices or teas. Hang pots on a pegboard on the wall, or hang them from wrought iron or wood ceiling fixtures. These fixtures will help free up counter space for food preparation or enable you to pot plants or dry herbs without feeling claustrophobic.

Try to plan the kitchen so that a window can be placed in the center of an exterior wall, preferably over the sink. This will let in a lot of natural light (especially if it faces south or east), give you a view, and create the leisure-time atmosphere that prompted you to build your house.

You can build an "open" kitchen, separated from a dining/living area by an island of cabinets and countertop. If you are dining informally you can sit on stools and eat at the countertop, freeing up more living space for other uses. In smaller cabins, kitchen appliances and cabinets might be located along one wall, with no physical separation of kitchen and dining areas.

MULTI-PURPOSE SPACES

Since your interior space is limited, make sure you use it efficiently. That means avoiding poor traffic patterns or classic "space wasters" like hallways. It also means using interior space for more than one purpose.

Bedrooms, for example, are not just for sleeping. If well designed, they can be used as hobby rooms, dens, or sitting rooms. Other living areas can provide additional sleeping space without appearing to be bedrooms.

You can finish off part of a living room wall, for example, with a small sleep center that looks like a sofa, surrounded by storage cubes that look like end tables, and backed by a plywood backrest and ledge that can be used to display plants or knick-knacks. At night, the full-sized bed can roll out to accommodate family members or guests.

You can build the cubes, backrest and ledge yourself. Place a bed lengthwise against the wall. Measure

Kitchen/dining areas can be separated by a room divider that also acts as buffet-server or countertop for informal dining. A window over the sink and range bring the outdoors "indoors." (Photo Courtesy of Champion Building Products)

desirable, equal widths next to the bed on each side for storage cubes. If you want to use the entire wall, the pieces have an attractive built-in look.

Use ¾ inch plywood for the cubes, topping each with a hinged lid. When stored in position against the back wall, the bed will be even with the fronts of the boxes.

The plywood and 2x4 framework for the ledge rests on the back edge of the two boxes. A board should be cut to fit between the two boxes, hinged at the top to form the backrest. You can top the ledge with plastic laminate, vinyl tile or ceramic tile to add visual interest.

The beauty of a vacation home is that you can create both dramatic and functional effects that might not be suitable for your primary home.

If your ceiling vaults to a height of 20 or 25 feet, for example, you can create extra space for sleeping, reading or conversation by building a loft.

Of course, you can get a simple wooden ladder to lead up to the loft space, but why not consider a spiral staircase? Knocked-down preassembled staircases made of wood or metal are available, and the cost will be lower than custom-built units or standard staircases. Loft areas are complemented by skylights or windows that let in natural light.

Multi-purpose rooms maximize space in vacation homes. The room shown here is used as a den, entertainment center or guest room. A pull-down Murphy bed hides in the wall, covered by plywood paneling. (Photo Courtesy of Champion Building Products)

Extra sleeping space created in and below loft area. Lofts can be built when ceilings vault to a height of 20 or 25 ft. (Photo Courtesy of Champion Building Products)

Indoor/outdoor living suits vacation retreats. Deck area off this living room could be used for eating in warm weather. (Photo courtesy of Champion Building Products)

Special attention should be paid to the ventilating, heating, and cooling of loft areas. Heat rises, and without proper ventilation these spaces can become intolerably warm.

Protective railing should be incorporated into the loft design: use wood or ordinary 1¼ inch pipe. If you have children, consider using some sort of protective device as guard railing to keep them from falling down the stairs.

PLANNING STORAGE SPACE

Homeowners and apartment dwellers agree that there never seems to be enough storage space. In a vacation home, that problem can easily lead to chaos! Storage space, both built-in and free-standing, can be strategically planned to bring order into your vacation world.

Let's start with the entryway. Since you are more likely to be bringing in bulky sports equipment like skis, fishing poles or golf clubs, and tracking in sand, mud, snow or other forms of dirt at the same time, a mudroom would be a welcome addition to your house plan. It could be designed with seating built around the perimeter of the room, to allow people to sit and comfortably remove wet things like flippers or ski boots before entering the main part of the home. Hooks and shelving in this room, too, will keep maintenance down by providing a single, orderly space in which to store boots, shoes, equipment and

outdoor clothing. In cold climates, the room can be heated with a warm-air floor furnace, which will help to dry outdoor gear. Galvanized or wooden-slatted grates over the subfloor in this room will allow you to scrape off mud or snow before you track it all over the house.

Let's move on to the main living area. A number of attractive possibilities are available to maximize storage. You can use wall space under windows for seating and storage units. This is somewhat difficult if you have expansive window space, however.

Built-in wall units in living areas accomplish two purposes: as interior decor and as handy places to store clothing, books, towels, sheets and other necessities. You can build the units yourself, or hire a carpenter. If you don't want or need a custom-built unit, there are many free-standing wall unit systems you can buy. They come in all styles, and components can be mixed to give your wall a custom look.

Wall units come in materials ranging from formica over particleboard or plywood to hardwood; costs vary too, from a few hundred dollars to several thousand dollars. Some free-standing systems come with "cap" units that fit over top components; standard height is 78 inches, and the "cap" units will bring the wall system up to a height of eight feet.

Look for unexpected spaces in your vacation home that might provide storage. Shelves or wall units can sometimes be used to good decorating and functional advantage on the wall under a staircase, for example. Don't overlook wall space over doors, either.

In A-frame houses, storage cabinets can be built into the wall and under the roof on the second floor loft area.

Ready-made storage cubes and baskets are ideal vehicles for attractive storage. The cubes can also serve as coffee tables, the baskets as design accents. If you make your own furniture, consider making couches that are really storage cubes, covered with plush padding or pillows. Baskets can accommodate the many small items that accumulate until they seem to overtake you: papers, pens, small toys, decks of cards, or household gadgets.

PLATFORMS—THE ULTIMATE BUILT-IN

The ultimate "built-in" is a platform system in the living area that provides storage, seating and even sleeping space. If your tastes are really modern, a multi-level platform design can even eliminate the need to buy other types of furniture such as chairs, sofas, or end tables.

You can incorporate a plywood platform eight to 12 inches high into your living-area design; build it to whatever length suits your purposes. The platform can be built along one wall of the room, possibly under a window. For storage add drawers along the perimeter of the platform; additional storage in the interior part can be made accessible with lift-up covers. On top of the basic platform, you may want to line the wall with plywood storage cubes of perhaps 18-inch height with lift-up covers.

These stepped platforms can be covered with an industrial grade carpeting, which wears well. Once decorated with colorful pillows the platform can serve as functional seating space, or as additional sleeping space for the truly hardy. A platform system using plywood and industrial-grade carpeting, can be installed for about $1,000 to $1,500.

MORE STORAGE SPACE

You can use the space in between interior wall studs for storage. It's easier to plan for this type of space before construction has begun, rather than after the house has been finished.

For the kitchen and bathroom, recessed cabinets with adjustable shelving can be inserted and nailed into the space between the studs.

In the living area, you can add bin storage space, starting at floor level, to hold extra table leaves (so that you can plan on using your table at its full length for buffets or other parties) in between the studs.

Normally, studs are spaced 16 inches apart; however, if you cut away a portion of one stud, (on a non-loadbearing wall) you can store leaves as large as 27 inches wide.

To do this, make a header, and cut away the part of the stud that extends below the header line. Sandwich a piece of ½ inch plywood between two 2x4s to make the header. Nail the header between the two studs around the opening, then nail a vertical 2x4 between each end of the header and floor.

To improve the appearance of the storage area, enclose it with plywood, frame the bin with 1x2s, and add a hinged door that will complement the rest of the wall material.

ROOM DIVIDERS

If the totally open living area design is not to your liking, you might want to create a room divider which can also function as a storage unit. Several room divider plans, suitable for living/dining areas or living areas/sleeping alcoves, are available from the American Plywood Association, 119 A Street, Tacoma, Washington 98401.

In the bedrooms, efficient use of space starts with the closets. Here are a few tips to give you the most storage space in your closets:

- Make walk-in closets wide enough for storage on both sides.

- Install hooks, racks or shelves on the back of closet doors.

- Make shelves adjustable.

- Use double rods where possible, to increase hanging space.

- Use ready-made organizers: stacks of plastic boxes or wire racks for shoes; multi-purpose garment hangers.

Wall units are suitable for bedrooms, too. They can be used instead of standard dressers and armoires, which take up more space. Either place them opposite the bed, or work them into the wall space around the bed. The latter eliminates the need for buying separate night tables.

Some platform beds come with built-in storage, too, as do some single beds and bunk beds. Stores specializing in unpainted furniture are a good source for these types of beds.

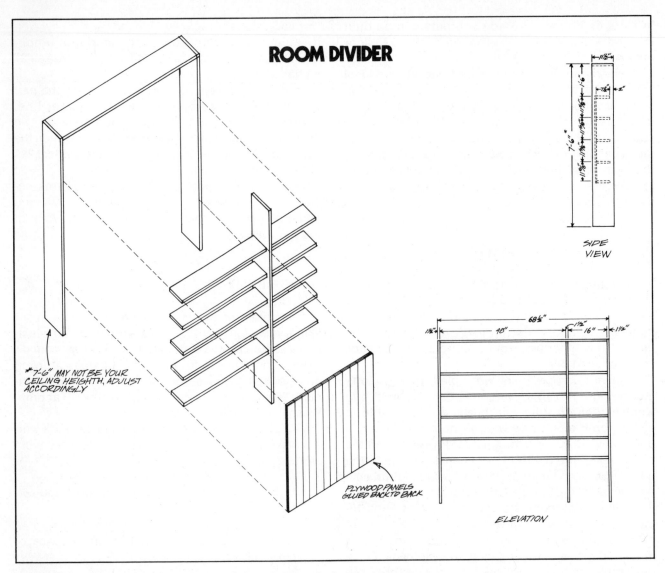

ROOM DIVIDER

*7'-6" MAY NOT BE YOUR CEILING HEIGHT, ADJUST ACCORDINGLY

PLYWOOD PANELS GLUED BACK TO BACK

SIDE VIEW

ELEVATION

This room divider can also be used for storage. Schematic drawing shows measurements. (Art courtesy of American Plywood Association)

MATERIALS FOR MINIMUM MAINTENANCE

The interior of a vacation home should be designed for minimum upkeep. Materials that require constant attention and cleaning, or that are susceptible to deterioration from gritty sand, mildew or extreme sunlight, will cause unnecessary grief in a vacation home.

Unfinished wood such as cedar, knotty pine or redwood can be used as interior finishes to create a warm atmosphere that will also provide years of low-maintenance use.

In flooring material, choose a covering that is durable and easy to clean, such as vinyl asbestos tile (particularly for high-use areas). You can cover floors with area rugs for high-fashion, low-cost look.

In the kitchen, using formica for countertops will prove to be economical and simple to maintain. Open shelving in the kitchen adds low-cost storage space but must be dusted more frequently than standard cabinets.

LIGHTING

The house will not be complete unless provisions are made for interior lighting. Where intensive lighting is needed, as in the kitchen, use fluorescents. They use less energy than incandescent fixtures, and will last far longer.

In living areas and bedrooms, wall-hung exposed white bulbs can be used effectively. They will give off a lot of light, and little glare. Dimmer controls for

Use materials that will keep maintenance chores to a minimum. Shown here is the bathroom area of a remodeled barn in Napa County, California. (Photo courtesy of California Redwood Association)

In this "L" shaped kitchen area, natural light has been used to its fullest. (Photo Courtesy of California Redwood Association)

these will extend their life and cut down on electricity costs. Low-cost "industrial" style hanging fixtures can also be used to good effect for accent lighting in conversation and dining areas.

You can cut down on the number of lighting fixtures needed in your home, however, by taking advantage of natural light. The amount of light coming in depends on the amount of sky visible through the window, so the higher the window area, the more natural illumination there will be.

Domed skylights that are insulated will diffuse natural light over a broad area. They will also reduce heat transmission, and therefore lower heat gain, during the summer. In the winter, when sun angles are lower, they have better light transmission than flat skylights. Domed skylights are available in venting units, allowing for natural ventilation.

Skylights can be effectively positioned in living/dining areas, kitchens or bathrooms. For instructions on how to add a skylight, see Chapter 5.

10
Protecting Your Vacation Home

Protecting your vacation home is no easier than protecting your primary residence; in fact, it is more difficult because much of the time the unit is not occupied. Also, it is usually in a secluded area where it is harder for local authorities to keep a close watch. Protection of the dwelling should begin with the first shipment of materials to the building site.

THE BUILDING SITE

Even in far away, serene surroundings, thefts can take place. If you leave building materials and tools unprotected at your vacation home-building site, you are asking for trouble. Building materials have a habit of getting up and "walking" away between the two weekends that you are on the building site.

The best way to avoid problems is to leave nothing at the site that has not been "nailed down": If you are building the house yourself, you should only take delivery of materials which you will use at that particular time. This is not always possible, but you should try to follow this ground rule.

After excavation, you will have to order concrete block. These can usually be left out in the open; a thief would have to labor long and hard to steal them. And if they are removed, cost of replacement would not be that great. What you do not want to leave there unprotected is a mechanical concrete mixer. This is an expensive item to replace. If you rent one for a long period of time, chain it and lock it around a thick tree on the building site.

If you are building a house on a concrete block crawl space or a full foundation, get the block in place as quickly as possible. Immediately try to get the bottom platform in place, then put a door on the foundation area. This can be an excellent space to store items. It is not 100 percent effective in preventing losses, but it certainly will help. This secured area is a good place for wheel barrows, shovels and other such items—but not for easily removed and expensive tools. Put those in the trunk of your car, and take them to and from the site as you need to use them.

If you are having a contractor build your house, then he will be responsible for all materials and his own tools. It is best to create a contract with him making him responsible for materials and labor. This is slightly more costly, but if you buy the materials separately from the contract, then the burden of protection is on you.

When building the house yourself, you will have a lumber list so that you can estimate costs. A word of caution: do not take delivery of all lumber at once. For

Intruder/fire alarm system can be built into vacation home. Any tampering with fire-heat detectors, smoke detectors or breaks in wiring, interrupts flow of current and results in alarm signals sounding. (Photo courtesy of NuTone Division, Scovill)

purposes of getting the best deal on costs, you can negotiate a package price with the lumber yard. But have them make deliveries in small quantities. That way, if a theft occurs you lose a portion but not all of your lumber. If you are a weekend builder, take the time Sunday afternoon to put away as much of the materials as you can.

Once the superstructure has been completed, put all windows and doors in place and lock them securely. Besides thieves, building sites are also subject to vandals—often youngsters from the area who have nothing better to do than work mischief on your labor of love.

Passersby have a fascination for partially-built homes and when no one is at the site, they like to walk through the project. Of course, if someone is injured, you are responsible. Therefore, have adequate insurance from the time you begin the project. Usually you need a contractor's liability policy while construction is underway, which then converts to a homeowner's policy on completion.

Leave nothing around the building site with which a vandal could do damage. One recent example is a do-it-yourself builder who left 10-gallon cans of thick, black concrete waterproofing material out in the open. He figured it was safe because the material would not cost much to replace.

What he did not count on was young vandals who poured the waterproofing cement all over the bottom platform, the siding and filled barrels of nails with the liquid. By the time he arrived at the site a week later, everything was solidified. He had insurance which reinbursed him for the damage, but he lost a whole weekend cleaning up. Therefore, do not leave paint, varnish, acid, gasoline or any type of spray can around where someone can use it against you.

As construction proceeds, do not leave expensive windows, cabinets or any appliance in the house but not installed for any longer than necessary.

You will need electricity at the site at the start of the construction process in order to operate power tools. It is advisable to set up lights with timers so that as darkness falls, the house can be lighted. This is more necessary once the superstructure has been completed than while it is partially built. Also, notify local authorities that the house is being constructed. Although the police cannot keep constant watch on the site, they will cooperate and drive past it several times a day. At times when no one is working at the site, they should be so notified. That way, if an unauthorized person is there and the police see him, they can take action. Further, leave a telephone number with the local authorities so you can be reached during the week.

PROTECTING THE FINISHED HOUSE

There's no way to assure absolute protection of your vacation home or belongings while you are not there. Although windows and doors can be locked, windows and doors can also be broken. But a good idea is to use well-made security hardware that will not only protect the home while you are not there, but also while you are there.

Lights connected to timers are an excellent idea once the house has been finished and furnished. Some people even connect a television set or radio to a timer so that as darkness falls there are not only lights on in the house, but also noise. This can make the dwelling appear occupied and help discourage entry.

When you are not going to be at the house for long periods of time, it is best to remove valuables, whether an antique quilt or rocking chair or your favorite painting. If the house is broken into and robbed, you will want to minimize your loss as much as possible.

At times when you are there frequently, such as every weekend, you might risk leaving your fishing gear, but you should not leave $1,000 worth of camera equipment, a new $500 color television or your rare gold coin collection; common sense should be exercised.

ANIMALS

If your new house is off in the woods, you will have to protect it from other intruders—animals. Thus, if there is nothing in your cabin worth stealing, you will still want to secure it. A raccoon which gets into your house can cause a big mess. He or she will open every cabinet, sample all of your food, and in general cause a mess. For the same reaons you will also want to keep any trash under lock and key. A latch is not good enough because a raccoon or other animals are smart enough to open latches.

Smaller animals such as rodents and termites can also wreak havoc while you are away from your vacation home.

Rodents generally have two ways of entering the house: underneath a foundation or through the flues. How can you prevent these little devils from seeking shelter in your home? Concrete foundations are better than other types for this purpose.

As for flues, they should be capped tightly if you are closing the home for an extended period of time. Materials need not be fancy; a metal hood will do, or wire

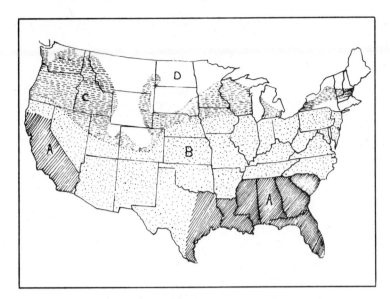

TERMITE SUSCEPTIBILITY BY GEOGRAHIC AREA
A. Region I (including Hawaii): termite protection required.
B. Region II: termite protection generally required, although specific areas sometimes exempted.
C. Region III: termite protection usually not required, except specific local areas.
D. Region IV (including Alaska): termite protectin not required.
SOURCE: U.S. Department of Housing and Urban Development (HUD) Minimum Property Standards. Washington, D.C.: Government Printing Office.

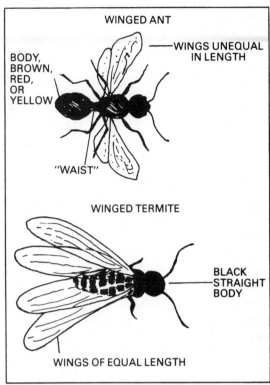

Winged ants are commonly mistaken for winged termites. Differences are noted in sketch.

screens. If your stove pipe is not hooded, that should be capped. Dampers should also be closed.

Don't give animals any additional incentive to gnaw their way into your home. Remove all opened food and liquids. Besides spoilage or burst containers, left-over food will attract all kinds of animals and insects; this includes dry foods like cereals.

You will want to store bedding away for extended periods of time regardless of whether or not you think you would have a rodent problem. As a safeguard, store bedding inside bunk frames or storage boxes lined with metal.

TERMITES

The object of a termite colony is to feast on the wood in your house; preferably, wood that is decaying, in an environment of warm temperature and high soil moisture. Subterranean termites, responsible for the greatest percentage of termite damage in the U.S., build nests and "subway systems" well below frost line, near their food supply—the house.

Their tunnels are continuous and clear cut. And, just as a subway system has underground and above-ground paths, so do termites. If the path to the wood is interrupted by an impermeable surface, they will build a small mud "tube" to the wood. Once they reach their goal, your flooring, studding, window and door frames are all vulnerable.

While your house is being built, consider these measures to dissuade termites from becoming occupants.

- Have the soil treated with a poison at the building site; a professional should do this.

- Use preservative-treated wood for parts of the superstructure subject to termite invasion.

- Use metal casings for basement windows and doors.

- Remove all dead wood and stumps from areas of the building site near the house—don't just bury them.

- If you have a crawl space instead of a full foundation, install an access window and ventilation. Closed off areas under house should be avoided.

How do you know if your house is feeding a termite colony? Unfortunately, in many cases you wouldn't

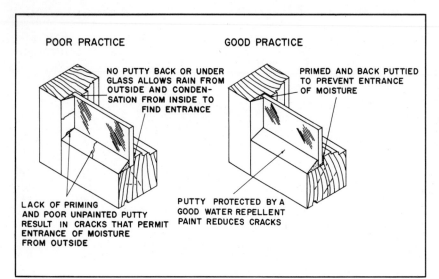

POOR PRACTICE   GOOD PRACTICE

NO PUTTY BACK OR UNDER GLASS ALLOWS RAIN FROM OUTSIDE AND CONDENSATION FROM INSIDE TO FIND ENTRANCE

PRIMED AND BACK PUTTIED TO PREVENT ENTRANCE OF MOISTURE

LACK OF PRIMING AND POOR UNPAINTED PUTTY RESULT IN CRACKS THAT PERMIT ENTRANCE OF MOISTURE FROM OUTSIDE

PUTTY PROTECTED BY A GOOD WATER REPELLENT PAINT REDUCES CRACKS

Window sash should be primed and back-puttied before glazing. Otherwise cracks will develop, permitting moisture to come in from outside, and condensation to build up on the inside. (U.S. Dept. of Agriculture)

know until you notice that, for example, a floor joist is sagging.

Look for termite tubing in the basement or crawl space. If tubes are moist, a colony is in residence below your home. If the tubes are dry and brittle, it may have already gone to greener pastures.

Also, keep checking for cracks in the foundation, or loose mortar, where termites might enter. The termites that make their forays into the wood to bring food back to the colony can penetrate a masonry crack of 1/64 of an inch wide.

If you can push the point of a small knife or screwdriver about a half-inch into any of the wood in the basement, it may be a sign of trouble. Don't keep piles of papers lying around, either, because that is an alternate meal for termites.

In the event that your home does suffer any termite infestation, your best bet would be to call in a professional exterminator or to chemically treat the house. You should also get a guarantee of at least a year that you won't be bedeviled by termites following the exterminator's work. Annual inspections are a good idea.

FUNGI

Fungi are microscopic plants that can devastate wood. Some fungi only discolor wood, while "decay fungi" destroy fiber. Fungi cannot work in dry wood; they need wood that contains 20 percent moisture. Sometimes, fungi and soil-nesting termites work in the same wood.

To prevent decay, keep the fungi from entering the lower part of the house. When the house is built, dry wood should be used, and wood should be kept dry during the building process as much as possible.

Also keep in mind that the sapwood of all species of trees is susceptible to decay, whereas heartwood is more durable. Woods that are treated with a preservative are more decay-resistant.

Roof design can also help prevent decay. An overhang of 12 inches on a one-story house is effective. If there are no overhanging eaves, gutters and downspouts are desirable. Wood surfaces like windows and doors should be flashed with a noncorroding metal.

No wood should be allowed to be in contact with soil unless the wood is thoroughly impregnated with the right preservative. Wood such as grade stakes, concrete forms, or stumps left on or in soil under houses also invites decay.

Listed are other factors that contribute to decay.

- Undrained soil and insufficient ventilation in homes that have no basements.

- Wood parts embedded in masonry near the ground.

- Use of infected lumber.

- Poor joinery around windows and doors and at corners and inadequate paint maintenance.

- Attics that are unventilated.

- Roof leaks, particularly around kitchen and laundry equipment and around shower/bathtubs.

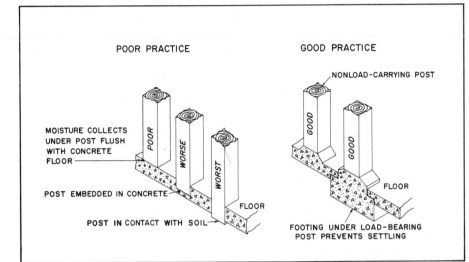

POOR PRACTICE

GOOD PRACTICE

NONLOAD-CARRYING POST

MOISTURE COLLECTS UNDER POST FLUSH WITH CONCRETE FLOOR

POOR

WORSE

WORST

GOOD

GOOD

FLOOR

POST EMBEDDED IN CONCRETE

POST IN CONTACT WITH SOIL

FLOOR

FOOTING UNDER LOAD-BEARING POST PREVENTS SETTLING

Installing wood directly into the soil or in concrete near the soil can easily lead to decay. Non-load-carrying posts should be set on raised concrete bases. (U.S. Dept. of Agriculture)

Smoke and heat detectors are either fixed-temperature or rate-of-rise mechanisms. A home should have at least one detector on each level of the house. (Courtesy of NuTone Division, Scovill)

Precautions should be taken at the time of construction. Proper maintenance must be practiced throughout the home's life, so be ever-watchful for leaky roofs, clogged drains, rust, "sweaty" pipes and more. If fungi are discovered, they should be traced back to their source of moisture, and the connection cut off. Sound, dry wood must be used to replace wood that has been hopelessly decayed, and if the infection has spread rapidly, then wood two feet in each direction from the decayed part should be removed and replaced, too. Before putting the new wood in place, all old wood and masonry surfaces around the decayed part should be brushed with a preservative.

PROTECTION FROM FIRE

A fire can be devastating to your home, whether or not you are in it at the time. While you are in the house, take these precautions: Be careful with matches and chemicals, particularly if there are children around. Do not smoke in bed; cigarettes and matches are the biggest contributors to home fires.

Be sure that electric wiring is safe and adequate. Electric circuits should be fused properly. Lightning rods should be properly installed and grounded as should arrestors on radio and television antennas. Periodically repair defective chimneys, spark arrestors, flues, stovepipes, and heating and cooking equipment if necessary. If you must store gasoline or other flammables, keep them in appropriate contain-

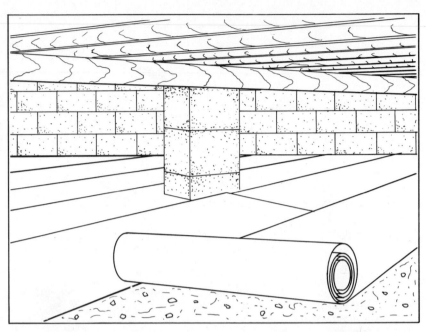

To keep soil moisture from vaporizing into the air and then condensing on joists and sills, cover soil under house with roll roofing. This technique also enables you to close crawl-space ventilators in winter. (U.S. Dept. of Agriculture)

ers and locations. Finally, consider installing fire detectors and smoke alarms in your vacation home, and keep a family-sized fire extinguisher on hand.

Because you will be away from your vacation home for extended periods of time, you will be very dependent on the watchfulness of your neighbors and the area fire department, if there is one. Do try to get to know your neighbors (even if they are far away from your home) and become acquainted with the firefighters who serve your area. This may be a county fire department, a volunteer department, special fire district, state Forestry Service or federal Forestry Service.

If you have a well for water, chances are it will be inadequate should the need arise for fire-fighting. You may need auxiliary water supplies, which can be in a tank or a pond. Fire trucks should be able to get within 20 feet of the auxiliary supply. You may also want to consider installing a rooftop sprinkler system, if water pressure is adequate.

PROTECTION FROM FLOODING

Whether your home is close to the ocean or nestled in the mountains, flooding from severe storms or thaws represents a serious threat.

There are several steps you can take to protect your home from flooding. If flooding is common in your area, consider stocking plastic sheeting, sandbags and lumber with which to build dikes around the house. Buy check valves from hardware or plumbing supply stores to keep water from backing up through sewer traps and drain pipes.

If flooding is forecast, get objects that are at ground level off that level by at least two or three feet. Keep underground fuel tanks filled, and seal them so that fuel oil won't spread over the property in case of a flood.

There is an insurance program called the National Flood Insurance Program, whose coverage comes from the Federal Housing and Urban Development Department. Not all communities qualify under the program, but you should check with a local property and casualty insurance agent. When a community first qualifies under the program, it is in emergency status. Once HUD sets premium rates, emergency status ends. Then you can get considerably more coverage on the house as well as on the contents than you can during the time the community is considered under emergency status.

Under normal circumstances, you should have a homeowners insurance policy that covers about 80 percent of the home's replacement cost. The mistake most people make is that they don't update their coverage to reflect realistic replacement costs. A home that cost $20,000 to build 10 years ago might cost twice that today, and so coverage of only $16,000 or so would not be much of a help if a calamity befalls the house.

You can include a clause in your policy that automatically escalates the coverage, or you can periodically have the house appraised to determine its current value, or work out some combination of the two. You can keep your premium costs down, at the same time, by increasing the amount of the deductible in the policy.

11
A Collection of Vacation-Home Plans

Here and on following pages are a selection of vacation home plans in which you might be interested. They are by no means the complete selection available from the companies which furnished them. In addition to the firms listed here, there are others around the country that create and furnish plans. Also, many shelter magazines publish "specials" which contain a wide variety of vacation home plans.

You can use these plans in a number of ways. First, you can obtain certain ideas from them which will spark your own ideas. Because most plans are really not very expensive, you can order a set of plans and even a materials list and study what's involved in the construction of a vacation home.

Once you have a set of plans before you, you can make what changes you desire and then take it to a local architect or engineer and have the plans "customized" as you wish. Or if you see a house and you like it just the way it is, lucky, you can work from there.

The one drawback to purchasing plans through the mail is that often a building department will not give you a building permit unless the plans are signed by a state-certified architect or engineer. Some plans companies might be able to help you overcome this problem by having professionals located within your state to help you.

Normally, however, you will have to find your own professional to sign the plans. This may or may not be a problem. Many architects, for example, do not want to be responsible for someone else's work. This is completely understandable. Therefore, if it is your intention to buy plans and use them as is, you might want to determine how you will get them signed before you purchase them.

Even if the building department in your area is not strict about this, a good idea nevertheless is to have a local professional go over the plans—especially if you intend to build the house yourself. That way, during the construction process, you will have someone to turn to for explanation of any design detail you may not fully understand.

Whether or not you use these plans for ideas or will actually build a unit shown here, they can be of enormous value in helping you get the vacation house you want, at a reasonable price.

The following Vacation Home plans are courtesy of *Home Plans, Inc.*. For further information on obtaining these or additional Vacation Home plans, write to this address: 23761 Research Drive, Farmington Hills, Michigan 48024.

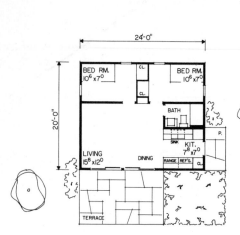

Design S 1486
480 Sq. Ft./4,118 Cu. Ft.

You'll be anxious to start building this delightful little vacation home. Whether you do-it-yourself, or engage professional help, you'll not have to wait long for its completion.

Design S 2425
1,106 Sq. Ft. / 14,599 Cu. Ft.

You'll adjust to living in this vacation cottage with the greatest of ease. And for evermore the byword will be, "fun". Imagine, a thirty-one foot living room!

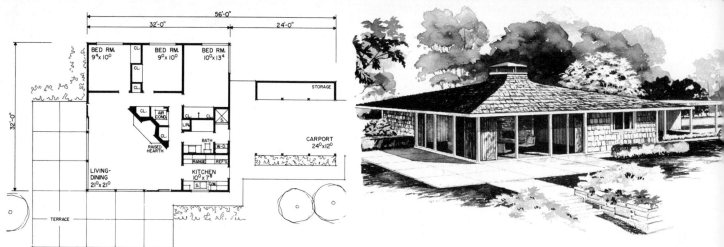

Design S 1449
1,024 Sq. Ft./11,264 Cu. Ft.

If yours is a preference for a vacation home with a distinctive flair, then you need not look any further. Here is a simple and economically built 32 foot rectangle.

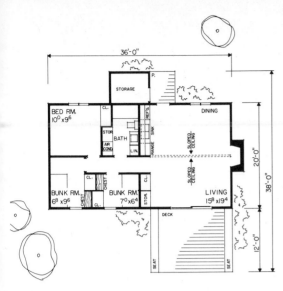

Design S 1488
720 Sq. Ft./8,518 Cu. Ft.

The kids won't be able to move into this vacation retreat soon enough. And neither will the housewife whose housekeeping will be almost non-existent. A real leisure-time home.

Design S 1462
1,176 Sq. Ft. / 11,995 Cu. Ft.

A second home with the informal living message readily apparent both inside and out. The zoning of this home is indeed most interesting — and practical, too. Study the plan carefully.

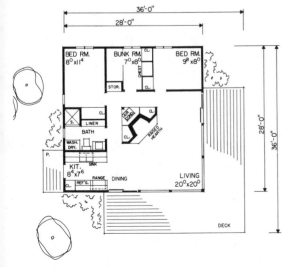

Here's a perfect 28 foot square that will surely open up new dimensions in living for its occupants. A fine, lower budget version of S 1449 on opposing page.

Design S 1485
784 Sq. Ft./10,192 Cu. Ft.

Design S 1453

1,476 Sq. Ft./13,934 Cu. Ft.

An exciting design, unusual in character, yet fun to live in. This frame home, with its vertical siding and large glass areas, has as its dramatic focal point a hexagonal living area which gives way to interesting angles. The large living area features sliding glass doors through which traffic may pass to the terrace stretching across the entire length of the house. The wide overhanging roof projects over the terrace and results in a large covered area outside the sliding doors of the master bedroom.

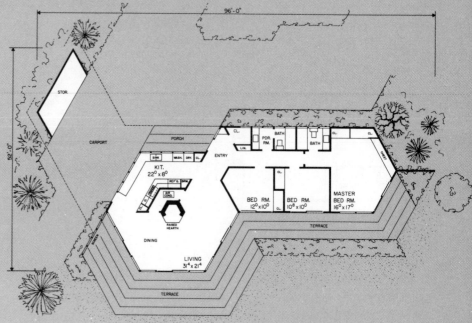

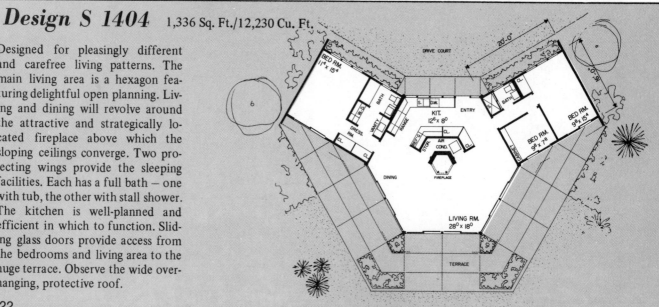

Design S 1404 1,336 Sq. Ft./12,230 Cu. Ft.

Designed for pleasingly different and carefree living patterns. The main living area is a hexagon featuring delightful open planning. Living and dining will revolve around the attractive and strategically located fireplace above which the sloping ceilings converge. Two projecting wings provide the sleeping facilities. Each has a full bath — one with tub, the other with stall shower. The kitchen is well-planned and efficient in which to function. Sliding glass doors provide access from the bedrooms and living area to the huge terrace. Observe the wide overhanging, protective roof.

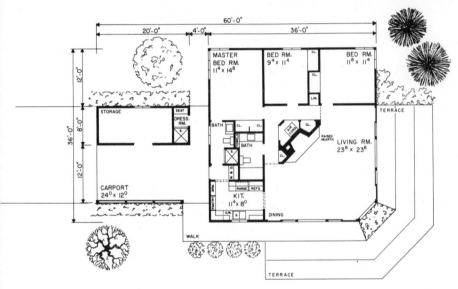

Design S 2457

1,288 Sq. Ft./13,730 Cu. Ft.

Leisure living will indeed be graciously experienced in this hip-roofed second home. Except for the clipped corner, it is a perfect square measuring 36 x 36 feet. The 23 foot square living room enjoys a great view of the surrounding environment by virtue of the expanses of glass. The wide overhanging roof affords protection from the sun. The "open planning" adds to the spaciousness of the interior. The focal point is the raised hearth fireplace. The three bedrooms are served by two full baths also accessible to other areas.

Design P 1499 /896 Sq. Ft.—Main Level/298 Sq. Ft.—Upper Level/896 Sq. Ft.—Lower Level/18,784 Cu. Ft.

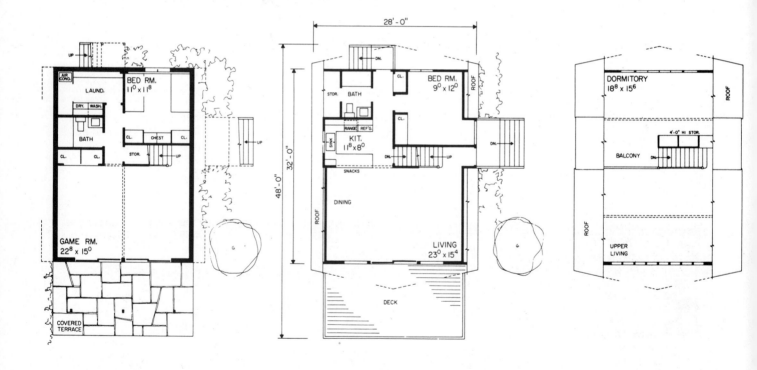

Three level living results in family living patterns which will foster a delightful feeling of informality. Upon his arrival at this charming second home, each family member will enthusiastically welcome the change in environment—both in-

doors and out. Whether looking down into the living room from the dormitory balcony, or walking through the sliding doors onto the huge deck, or participating in some family activity in the game room, everyone will count the hours spent

here as relaxing ones. Study the plan carefully. Note the sleeping facilities on each of the three levels. There are two full baths, a separate laundry room, and plenty of storage. Don't miss the efficient U-shaped kitchen.

Appendix A
Glossary

Anchor bolts—bolts which secure the wood sill plate to the foundation wall.

Attic ventilators—either static or mechanical devices to move air in and out of attic. Vents are needed in this place to prevent heat and moisture build up.

Backfill—replacement of earth against house foundation.

Batten—strips of wood used to cover joints or as decorative vertical members over plywood or wide boards.

Batter boards—horizontal strips of wood nailed to stakes set at the corners of an excavation. These boards are used to indicate the desired level. When strings are attached, they also help outline the foundation walls.

Beam—structural member transversely supporting a load.

Bearing partition—a partition in a house or other structure which supports any vertical load and its own weight.

Brace—a piece of lumber which when applied to a wall or floor will help stiffen the structure. Temporary bracing is used in home construction to keep walls or other members steady and level while work proceeds.

Bridging—wood or metal members which are used in a perpendicular or diagonal position between joists at mid span to act both as tension and compression members to brace joists and spread the action of loads.

Butt joints—a joint where the ends of two pieces of lumber or other material meet in a square cut joint.

Collar beam—a wooden member, usually one or two inches thick, which is used to connect opposite roof rafters. Helps stiffen the roof rafters and entire structure.

Column—a vertical member used to support loads.

Condensation—droplets of water which condense from water vapor. Usually occurs in a house in an unventilated attic or basement. If condition persists, it can cause dry rot on wooden members.

Corner braces—diagonal braces which are applied at corners to help strengthen the wall.

Cornice—overhang of pitched roof at the eave line.

Crawl space—shallow space below house usually enclosed with foundation walls.

Crowning—term used to identify which way joists should be installed. Virtually every joist, on end, will have a slight warp. The side which warps up should be placed up. When plywood subflooring is applied the joist straightens out.

Dormer—an opening in the slope of the roof. The framing projects out and dormer end is suitable for a window. In small homes where there isn't much of a second floor, the addition of a single or double dormer can add to the living space of the house.

Downspout—pipe for carrying water from roof gutters.

Fascia—a horizontal board which is used as facing.

Footing—base for foundation walls, posts or chimneys, which is usually made of concrete. The footing is wider than the structure it supports in order to better distribute the weight over the ground to help prevent settling.

Gable—the triangular portion of the end wall of a house with a pitched roof.

Gussett—small piece of wood or metal which is attached to corners or intersections of a frame to add stiffness and strength.

Header—framing lumber used around opening to support free end of floor joists, studs or rafters.

Header Joist—horizontal lumber that butts against the ends of floor joists around the outside of the house to add strength and to tie joists together.

Joists—parallel framing members used to support floor or ceiling loads.

Molding—wood strip either rectangular or curved used for decorative purposes.

Non-load-bearing wall—an interior wall which does not support any weight other than its own.

O.c.—abbreviation for on center. Joists, rafters, wall studs are always positioned on center.

Outrigger—extension of rafter beyond wall line.

Panel—thin, flat piece of material used in house construction such as plywood and wallboard panels.

Paper, building—general term for all felts, papers and other materials used in house construction.

Partition—a wall which divides a space. Interior partition in house generally divides a space into two rooms.

Pier—a column, usually masonry but it could be of other materials, to help support other structural members.

Pitch—this indicates the incline or slope of a roof. The pitch of a roof is expressed in inches per foot.

Plate—general term used in construction. The sill plate is a horizontal member which is anchored by bolts usually to the foundation. In wall construction, there is one bottom plate and two top plates. The plates here are usually 2x4 on the horizontal which are nailed into wall studs.

Plumb—the exact perpendicular or vertical. When a wall is plumb it means that it is exactly vertical.

Ply—denotes the number of layers of a material.

Plywood—a piece of wood made with an odd number of layers of veneer. By gluing the wood veneers together, an incredibly strong material is created which far surpasses the natural material in strength.

Preservative—any substance which when applied to a material prevents that material from rot or decay.

Quarter round—molding which has the cross section of a quarter circle. It's often used as a molding.

Rafter—a structural member used to support the roof. When rafters are used on a flat roof they are often called roof joists.

Rafter hip—a structural member supporting the roof which forms the intersection of an external roof angle.

Reflective insulation—a sheet material such as aluminum foil with one or both sides of comparatively low heat conductivity.

Ribbon—a board horizontally on studs to support a ceiling or second-floor joists.

Ridge—the horizontal line at the top edge of a roof where two slopes meet.

Ridge board—board placed at the top of the ridge to which roof rafters are attached.

Rise—the vertical height of a step or flight of stairs.

Riser—vertical boards closing the spaces between the treads of stairs.

Roof sheathing—sheets of plywood or another material which is applied to roof rafters to enclose house. Roofing material is applied to roof sheathing usually after an underlayment is added.

Sash—a single light frame containing one or more panes of glass.

Saturated felt—felt impregnated with tar or asphalt used in construction.

Shake—a handsplit wood shingle.

Sheathing—structural covering used over rafters or studs. The material is usually lumber or plywood. Generally, walls and roofs today are sheathed with plywood panels.

Shingles—roof covering usually made of slate wood, asbestos or a variety of other materials.

Shingles, siding—an exterior wall covering generally made of wood shingles or shakes or other non-wood material.

Siding—on exterior walls it is the finish covering. Siding can be of any number of materials from plywood to lumber to non-wood materials.

Sill—the lowest member of the frame of a structure which generally sits on the concrete block foundation. Generally known as sill plates.

Sleeper—material, usually wood embedded in concrete to serve as a fastener and/or to support subfloor or flooring.

Span—the distance between structural supports such as walls or columns.

Square—as in a square of shingles. In construction it is a measurement of 100 square feet.

Stud—a vertical wall support member usually wood or metal. In frame construction, a series of 2x4 studs is the vertical support attached to one 2x4 bottom plate and two 2x4 top plates.

Termite shield—a metal sheet which prevents the passage of termites into the house. The material is usually put around foundation and pipes near ground level.

Trim—finish materials in a house such as moldings.

Truss—a frame designed to act as a beam over long spans.

Underlayment—any material placed under finished coverings such as shingles or flooring which provides a good surface for the finish.

Vapor barrier—any material which is used to retard the movement of moisture. Used in conjunction with insulation.

Weatherstripping—narrow sections of metal used around doors or windows to prevent air infiltration.

Appendix B
Federal Land Banks
& their Territories

The Federal Land Bank of Springfield
P.O. Box 141
Springfield, MA 01101
Maine, New Hampshire, Vermont, Massachusetts, Rhode Island, Connecticut, New York, and New Jersey

The Federal Land Bank of Baltimore
P.O. Box 1555
Baltimore, MD 21203
Pennsylvania, Delaware, Maryland, Virginia, West Virginia, District of Columbia, and Puerto Rico

The Federal Land Bank of Columbia
P.O. Box 1499
Columbia, SC 29202
North Carolina, South Carolina, Georgia, and Florida

The Federal Land Bank of Louisville
P.O. Box 239
Louisville, KY 40201
Ohio, Indiana, Kentucky, and Tennessee

The Federal Land Bank of New Orleans
P.O. Box 50590
New Orleans, LA 70150
Alabama, Mississippi, and Louisiana

The Federal Land Bank of St. Louis
Main P.O. Box 491
St. Louis, MO 63166
Illinois, Missouri, and Arkansas

The Federal Land Bank of St. Paul
375 Jackson Street
St. Paul, MN 55101
Michigan, Wisconsin, Minnesota, and North Dakota

The Federal Land Bank of Omaha
P.O. Box 1242
Omaha, NE 68101
Iowa, Nebraska, South Dakota, and Wyoming

The Federal Land Bank of Wichita
151 North Main
Wichita, KS 67202
Oklahoma, Kansas, Colorado, and New Mexico

The Federal Land Bank of Houston
P.O. Box 2649
Houston, TX 77001
Texas

The Federal Land Bank of Berkeley
P.O. Box 525
Berkeley, CA 94701
California, Nevada, Utah, Arizona, and Hawaii

The Federal Land Bank of Spokane
W. 705 First Avenue
Spokane, WA 99204
Washington, Oregon, Montana, Idaho, and Alaska

Appendix C
Manufacturer's Addresses

Fireplaces & Equipment, Glass & Glazing, Heating Systems, Humidifiers & Dehumidifiers, Insulation, Skylights, Solar Collectors & Devices, Ventilating Equipment, Water Heaters, Windows, Wind Power Equipment, Wood Burning Stoves

Fireplaces & Equipment

Cadet Mfg. Co.
2500 W. Fourth Plain Blvd.
Vancouver, WA 98663

Dura-Vent
2525 El Camino Real
Redwood City, CA 94064

Dyna Mfg. Co. Inc.
2540 Industry Way
Lynwood, CA 90262

Fasco Ind. Inc.
P.O. Box 150
Fayetteville, NC 28302

Heatilator Fireplace
Div. Vega Ind. Inc.
P.O. Box 409
Mt. Pleasant, IA 52641

Leigh Products Inc.
Coppersville, MI 49404

The Majestic Co.
245 Erie St.
Huntington, IN 46750

Malm Metal Products Inc.
2640 Santa Rosa Ave.
Santa Rosa, CA 95401

Martin Inc.
3414 Governors Drive
Huntsville, AL 35801

Preway Inc.
1430 Second St.
Wisconsin Rapids, WI 54494

Superior Fireplace Co.
P.O. Box 2066
4325 Artesia Ave.
Fullerton, CA 92633

U.S. Stove Co.
S. Pittsburgh, TN 37380

Vega Industries
P.O. Box 409
Mt. Pleasant, IA 52641

Washington Stove Works
P.O. Box 687
Everett, WA 98201

Glass & Glazing

ASG Industries Inc.
P.O. Box 929
Kingsport, TN 37662

DAP Inc.
P.O. Box 277
Dayton, OH 45401

Dearborn Glass Co.
6600 S. Harlem Ave.
Bedford Park, IL 60638

Libbey-Owens-Ford Co.
811 Madison Ave.
Toledo, OH 43695

PPG Industries
One Gateway Center
Pittsburgh, PA 15222

Pittsburgh, Corning Corp.
Three Gateway Center
Pittsburgh, PA 15222

Season All Industries
Indiana, PA 15701

Heating Systems

Addison Products Co.
P.O. Box 100
Addison, MI 49220

Ammark Corp.
12-22 River Rd.
Fairlawn, NJ 07410

Arkla Air Conditioning
Div. Arkla Ind. Inc.
400 E. Capital
Little Rock, AR 72203

Bryant Air Conditioning Co.
7310 W. Morris St.
Indianapolis, IN 46231

Cadet Mfg. Co.
2500 W. Fourth Plain Blvd.
P.O. Box 1685
Vancouver, WA 98663

Crane Co.
300 Park Ave.
New York, NY 10022

Day & Night Co.
855 Anaheim-Puente Rd.
La Puente, CA 91749

Emerson Electric Co.
Chromalox Comfort Condition Div.
8100 W. Florissant Ave.
St. Louis, MO 63136

Fasco Industries Inc.
P.O. Box 150
Fayetteville, NC 28302

Federal Pacific Electric Co.
150 Ave. L
Newark, NJ 07101

General Electric Co.
Appliance Park
Louisville, KY 40225

Heat Controller Inc.
1900 Wellworth Ave.
Jackson, MI 49203

Heil-Quaker Corp.
647 Thomason Lane
Nashville, TN 37204

Johnson Corp.
421 Monroe St.
Bellevue, OH 44811

Kewanee Boiler
101 Franklin St.
Kewanee, IL

Trane Co.
3600 Pammel Creek Rd.
La Crosse, WI 54601

Humidifiers & Dehumidifiers

Bryant Air Conditioning Co.
7310 W. Morris St.
Indianapolis, IN 46231

Dayton Electric Mfg. Co.
5959 W. Howard St.
Chicago, IL 60648

General Electric Co.
Appliance Park
Louisville, KY 40225

Heat Controller Inc.
1900 Wellworth Ave.
Jackson, MI 49203

Hermidifier Co. Inc.
P.O. Box 1747
Lancaster, PA 17604

Home Siegler Div.
Lear Siegler Inc.
15929 East Valley Blvd.
Industry, CA 91744

Leigh Products Inc.
Coopersville, MI 49404

Porter H.K. Co.
Porter Bldg.
Pittsburgh, PA 15219

Trane Co.
3600 Pammel Creek Rd.
La Crosse, WI 54601

Insulation

Celotex Corp.
1500 N. Dale Mabry
Tampa, FL 33607

Certain-Teed Products Corp.
Shelter Materials Group
P.O. Box 860
Valley Forge, PA 19482

DeVac, Inc.
10130 Highway 55
Minneapolis, MN 55441

E.I. Dupont,
Prod. Info. Section
1007 Market Street
Wilmington, DE 19898

Flintkote Co.
480 Central Ave.
E. Rutherford Ave., NJ 07073

General Aluminum Western Div.
4850 Irving Street
Boise, ID 83704

Globe Industries Inc.
2638 E. 126 St.
Chicago, IL 60636

Gold Bond Building Prod. Div.
National Gypsum Co.
325 Delaware Ave.
Buffalo, NY 14202

Grace, W. R. & Co.,
Construction Prod. Div.
62 Whittlemore Ave.
Cambridge, MA 02140

Homasote Co.
P.O. Box 240
W. Trenton, NJ 08628

Johns-Manville
Denver, CO 80217

National Cellulose Corp.
12315 Robin Blvd.
Houston, TX

National Gypsum Co.
325 Delaware Ave.
Buffalo, NY 12832

Norton Co.
Sealant Operations
Granville, NY 14202

Owens-Corning Fiberglas Corp.
Fiberglas Tower
Toledo, OH 43601

PPG Industries
One Gateway Center
Pittsburgh, PA 15222

Porter H.K. Company
Porter Bldg.
Pittsburgh, PA 15222

Season All Industries, Inc.
Indiana, PA 15701

Temple Ind.
Diboll, TX 74941

Therma-Coustics, Inc.
21900 Main St.
P.O. Box 190
Colton, CA 92324

Thermtron Prod. Inc.
P.O. Box 9146 Baer Field
Fort Wayne, IN 46809

U.S. Mineral Prods. Co.
Stanhope, NJ 07874

U.S. Plywood Div.
Champion-International
1 Landmark Sq.
Stamford, CT

Weyerhaeuser Co.
Tacoma, WA 98401

Skylights

Bell Skylights Div.
The Richard Grant Co.
2039 Pech Rd.
P.O. Box 55583
Houston, TX 77055

Cadillac Plastic & Chemical
15841 2 Ave.
Detroit, MI 48232

Dimensional Plastics Corp.
1065 E. 26 St.
Box 3337
Hialeah, FL 33013

Kosman Lighting Equipment Co.
2201 3rd St.
San Francisco, CA 94107

George C. Vaughan & Sons
223 S. Frio St.
San Antonio, TX 78207

Morgan-Wightman Supply Co.
Main P.O. Box 1
St. Louis, MO 63166

Solar Collectors & Devices

Arkla Ind. Inc.
950 E. Virginia St.
Evansville, IN 47701

Beutel Solar Heater Co.
1527 N. Miami Ave.
Miami, FL 33132

Edward's Engineering Corp.
101 Alexander Ave.
Pompton Plains, NJ 07444

Enthone, Inc.
Box 1900
New Haven, CT 06508

FAFCO
2860 Spring St.
Redwood City, CA 94063

Kalwall Corp.
P.O. Box 237
Manchester, NH 03105

Ram Products Co.
1111 N. Centerville Rd.
Sturgis, MI 49091

Solar Energy Co.
810 18 St., N.W.
Washington, DC 20006

Sunworks, Inc.
669 Boston Post Rd.
Guilford, CT 06437

Transparent Products Corp.
1727 W. Pico Blvd.
Los Angeles, CA 90015

Tranter Manufacturing Inc.
735 E. Hazel St.
Lansing, MI 48909

Ventilating Equipment

American Metal Products, Inc.
6100 Bandini Blvd.
Los Angeles, CA 90040

Aubrey Mfg. Co.
Union, IL 60180

Broan Mfg. Co. Inc.
P.O. Box 140
Hartford, WI 53027

Butler Engineering Co.
P.O. Box 728
Mineral Wells, TX 76067

Distinctive Appliances
7251 Hinds Ave.
N. Hollywood, CA 91605

Fasco Industries, Inc.
P.O. Box 150
Fayetteville, NC 28302

General Electric Co.
Appliance Park
Louisville, KY 40225

Glenwood Range Co.
140 Industrial Park
Taunton, MA 02780

Goodwin of California, Inc.
1075 Second St.
Berkeley, CA 94710

Gray & Dudley Co.
2300 Clifton Rd.
Nashville, TN 37209

H.C. Products Co.
Box 68
Princeville, IL 61159

ILG Industries, Inc.
2850 N. Pulaski Rd.
Chicago, IL 60641

Jensen Ind.
1946 East 46
Los Angeles, CA 90058

Kich-N-Vent Div.,
Home Metal Prod. Co.
750 Central Expressway
Plano, TX 75074

Kool-O-Matic Corp.
1831 Terminal Rd.
Niles, MI 49120

Leslie Locke Bldg. Prod. Co.
Ohio St.
Lodi, OH 44254

Louver Mfg. Co. Inc.
P.O. Box 519
2101 W. Main St.
Jacksonville, AR 72076

Modern Maid, Inc.
E. 14 St.
Chattanooga, TN 37301

Morgan-Wightman Supply Co.
Main P.O. Box 1
St. Louis, MO 63166

National Industries Inc.
1410 S.W. 12th Ave.
P.O. Box 293
Ocala, FL 32670

NuTone Div., Scovill Mfg. Co.
Madison & Red Bank Rds.
Cincinnati, OH 45227

Penn Ventilator Co. Inc.
11th St. & Allegheny Ave.
Philadelphia, PA 19140

Power Vent
185 E. South St.
Freeland, PA 18224

Rangaire Corp.
P.O. Box 177
Cleburne, TX 76031

Roper Sales
1905 W. Court
Kankakee, IL 60901

Sunray Stove Co.
Div. of Glenwood Range Co.
435 Park Ave.
Delaware, OH 43015

Thermador
Div. of Norris Industries
5119 District Blvd.
Los Angeles, CA 90022

Vent-A-Hood Co.
P.O. Box 426
Richardson, TX 75080

Water Heaters

Bryan System
Bryan Steam Corp.
P.O. Box 27
Peru, IN 46970

Dayton Elec. Mfg. Co.
5959 W. Howard St.
Chicago, IL 60648

Hydrotherm Inc.
Rockland Ave.
Northvale, NJ 07647

Megatherm Corp.
803 Taunton Ave.
E. Providence, RI 02914

Patterson-Kelley Co., Inc.
100 Burson St.
E. Stroudsburg, PA 18301

Precision Parts Corp.
400 No. 1st St.
Nashville, TN 37207

Rheem Mfg. Co.
Water Heating Products Div.
7600 South Kedzie Ave.
Chicago, IL 60652

A.O. Smith Corp.
Consumer Products Div.
Box 28
Kankakee, IL 60901

The Whalen Co.
Brock Bridge Rd.
Laurel, MD 20810

Windows

ALCOA
1501 Alcoa Bldg.
Pittsburgh, PA 15219

Allastics Div.,
Sub. of Bethlehem Steel
1275 Enterprise Drive
Narcross, GA 30071

Alsar, Inc.
21121 Telegraph Rd.
Southfield, MI 48075

American Alum Window Corp.
767 Eastern Ave.
Malden, MA 02148

Anderson Corp.
Bayport, MN 55003

Burton Wood Work
Burton Enterprises Inc.
Mac Arthur Ave.
Cobleskill, NY 12043

Capitol Prod. Corp.
P.O. Box 69
Mechanicsburg, PA 17055

Caradco Window & Door Div.
Scovill Mfg. Co.
1098 Jackson St.
Dubuque, IA 52001

Carmel Steel Prods.
13821 Marquardt Ave.
Santa Fe Springs, CA 90670

Certain-Teed Products Corp.
Ideal Co. Div.
Box 889
Waco, TX 76703

Crossly Window
7375 N.W. 35th Ave.
Miami, FL 33147

DeVac, Inc.
10130 Highway 55
Minneapolis, MN 55441

General Aluminum Western Div.
4850 Irving St.
Boise, ID 83704

International Window Corp.
5626 E. Firestone Blvd.
S. Gate, CA 90280

Kawneer Co.
1105 N. Front St.
Niles, MI 49120

Keller Ind. Inc.
18000 St. Rd. 9
Miami, FL 33162

Louisiana-Pacific Corp.
Weather-Seal Div.
324 Wooster Rd. North
Barbeton, OH 44203

Malta, A Division of Philips Industries
P.O. Box 397
Malta, OH 43758

Marvin Windows
Warroad, MN 56763

Mon-Ray Windows, Inc.
6118 Wayzata Blvd.
Minneapolis, MN 55416

Norton Co.
Sealant Operations
Granville, NY 12832

The Pease Co.
900 Forest Ave.
Hamilton, OH 45012

Ponderosa Pine Woodwork
Yeon Bldg.
Portland, OR 97204

R.O.W. Window Sales Co.
1365 Academy Ave.
Ferndale, MI 48220

Remington Aluminum
Div. of Evans Prods.
100 Andrews Rd.
Hicksville, NY 11801

Reynolds Metals Co.
325 West Touhy Ave.
Park Ridge, IL 60068

Rimco Div., Rodman Industries
P.O. Box 97
Rock Island, IL 61201

Maratta Productions, Inc.
992 Wethersfield Ave.
Hartford, CT 06114

Portland Stove Foundry Co.
57 Kennebec St.
Portland, ME 04104

Scandinavian Stoves, Inc.
Box 72
Alstead, NH 03602

Rolscreen Co.
100 Main St.
Pella, IA 50219

Rusco Ind. Inc. Rusco Division
Box 124
Cochronton, PA 16314

Season All Ind., Inc.
Indiana, PA 15701

Geo. C. Vaughan & Sons
223 S. Frio St.
San Antonio, TX 78207

Winter Seal of Flint, Inc.
209 Elm St.
Holly, MI 48442

Zegers, Inc.
16727 Chicago Ave.
Lansing, IL 60438

Wind Power Equipment

Aeromotor Div. of Brader Ind.
800 E. Dallas St.
Broken Arrow, OK 74012

Automatic Power, Inc.
Pennwalt Corp.
205 Hutcheson St.
Houston, TX 77003

Bucknell Engineering Co.
10717 E. Rush St.
El Monte, CA 91733

Dyna Technology Inc.
P.O. Box 3263
Sioux City, IA 51102

O'Brock Windmill Sales
Rte. 1, 12 St.
North Benton, OH 44449

Wood Burning Stoves

Automatic Draft & Stove Co.
Lynchburg, VA 24500

Birmingham Stove and Range Co.
P.O. Box 2593
Birmingham, AL 35202

Brown Stove Works, Inc.
Cleveland, TN 37311

C&D Distributors, Inc.
P.O. Box 715
Old Saybrook, CT 06475

King Stove and Range Co.
P.O. Box 730
Sheffield, AL 35660

Kristia Associates
P.O. Box 1461
Portland, ME 04104

L.W. Gay Stove Works, Inc.
Marlboro, VT 05344

The Majestic Co., Inc.
Huntington, IN 46750

United States Stove Co.
South Pittsburg, TN 37380

Vermont Castings, Inc.
Randolph, VT 05060

Vermont Woodstove Co.
Bennington, VT 05201

Appendix D
Manufactured
Vacation Homes

Acorn Structures, Inc.
Box 250 Concord, MA 01742

American Barn Corp.
182
So. Deerfield, MA 01373

American Geodesic, Inc.
Box 164
Hampden Highlands, ME 04445

Authentic Homes
P.O. Box 1288
Laramie, WY 82070

Barn Homes
P.O. Box 579
Woodstock, NY 12498

Best Panel Homes
11301 Paddy's Run Rd.
Hamilton, OH 45013

Boise Cascade Mfg. Housing
Kingsberry Homes
61 Perimeter Park
Atlanta, GA 30341

Burkin Homes Corp.
White Pigeon, MI 49099

Cathedralite Domes
P.O. Box 880
Aptos, CA 95003

Cedar Forest Products Co.
Polo, IL 61064

Cluster Shed
Hartland, VT 05048

Custom Builders Corp.
3739 S. Lindbergh
St. Louis, MO 64050

Deck House, Inc.
930 Main St.
Acton, MA 01720

Domes and Homes, Inc.
P.O. Box 365
Brielle, NJ 08730

Flexi-Panel Corp.
1000 E. Apache Blvd.
Tempe, AZ 85281

Habitat
123 Elm St.
Deerfield, MA 01373

Hammond Barns
Box 584
New Castle, IN 47362

Hexagon Housing Systems, Inc.
905 N. Flood
Norman, OK 73069

Justus Co., Inc.
P.O. Box 91515
Tacoma, WA 98491

Lindal Cedar Homes
P.O. Box 24426
Seattle, WA 98124

Nor-Wes Cedar Chalets, Ltd.
915 W. 1st
N. Vancouver, B.C.

Pan Adobe Cedar Homes
4350 Lake Washington Blvd.
North Renton, WA 98055

Richmond Homes, Inc.
1325 Bridge Ave.
Richmond, IN 47374

Serendipity Shelter Systems
Pier 9, Embarcadero
San Francisco, CA 94111

Shelter-Kit Inc.
Franklin, NH 03235

Spacemakers, Inc.
146 Will Dr.
Canton, MA 02021

Stanmar, Inc.
Boston Post Rd.
Sudbury, MA 01776

Tension Structures (''O' Dome'')
9800 Ann Arbor Rd.
Plymouth, MI 48170

Trifold Homes
P.O. Box 4091
Incline Village, NV 89450

Vacation Land Homes, Inc.
P.O. Box 292
Bellaire, MI 49615

Wausau Homes, Inc.
P.O. Box 1204
Wausau, WI 54401

Weston Homes, Inc.
P.O. Box 126
Rotschild, WI 54474

Wickes Lumber Div. Wickes Corp.
P.O. Box 3244
Saginaw, MI 48605

Yankee Barn Homes, Inc.
Grantham, NH 03753

Appendix E
Log Cabin Kit
Manufacturers

Air-Lock Log Co., Inc.
P.O. Box 2506
Las Vegas, NM 87701

Alpine Log Homes
Box 85
Victor, MT

Alta Ind. Ltd.
P.O. Box 88
Halcottsville, NY 12438

American Timber Home
Escanaba, MI

Beaver Log Homes
Box 1145
Claremore, OK 74017

Belleaire Log Cabins
Box 322
Bellaire, MI 49615

Boyne Falls Log Homes
Boyne Falls, MI 49713

Building Logs, Inc.
P.O. Box 300
Gunnison, CO 81230

Carolina Log Buildings, Inc.
Box 363
Fletcher, NC 28732

Crockett Log Homes
Chesterfield, NH

Green Mountain Cabins, Inc.
Box 190
Chester VT 05143

Hamill Mfg. Co.
Grand Lodge, MI

Modelog
Lumber Enterprises Inc.
Box 1221
Billings, MT

National Beauti-Log Co.
1205 South Wilson Way
Stockton, CA 95205

National Log Co.
Thompson Falls, MT 59873

New England Log Homes, Inc.
Hampden, CT 06518

Northeastern Log Homes, Inc.
Kenduskeag, ME 04450

Northern Products, Inc.
Bangor, ME 04401

Pan-Adobe Inc.
4350 Lake Washington Blvd., N.
Renton, WA 98055

Pritchard Products Corp.
Timberlodge Div.
4625 Roanoke Pkwy.
Kansas City, MO 64112

R&L Log Building Inc.
Mount Upton, NY 13809

Real Log Homes, Inc.
Box 1520
Missoula, MT 59807

The Rustics of Lindbergh Lake
Seeley Lake, MT 59868

Shelterwood Co.
Box 100
Summit Lake, WI 54485

Timmerman Lumber & Mfg. Co.
Hibbing, MN

True Log Building
Box 50
Jonesboro, ME 04648

Universal Homes and Wood Products
3500 Guardian Bldg.
Detroit, MI

Vermont Log Buildings, Inc.
Hartland, VT 05048

Ward Cabin Co.
Houlton, ME 04730

Wilderness Log Homes
Rte. 2
Plymouth, WI 53073

Appendix F
Stock House
Plan Sources

Home Planners, Inc.
23761 Research Drive
Farmington, MI 48024

Garlinghouse Company
2320 Kansas Ave., Box 299
Topeka, Kansas 66601

Heritage Homes Plan Service, Inc.
Dept. 106, Suite 307
3030 Peachtree Rd., N.W.
Atlanta, GA 30305

Home Building Plan Service
Studio 28J
2235 Northeast Sandy Blvd.
Portland, OR 97232

National Plan Service
435 West Fullerton
Elmhurst, IL 60126

Master Plan Service, Inc.
89 East Jericho Tpke.
Mineola, NY 11501

Index